WORK
Types

JEAN M. KUMMEROW,
NANCY J. BARGER,
LINDA K. KIRBY

BUSINESS
PLUS

NEW YORK   BOSTON

Business Plus
Hachette Book Group
237 Park Avenue
New York, NY 10017

www.hachettebookgroup.com

Business Plus is an imprint of Grand Central Publishing.
The Business Plus name and logo are trademarks of Hachette Book Group, Inc.

Printed in the United States of America

First Edition: March 1997

10 9

Library of Congress Cataloging-in-Publication Data

Kummerow, Jean M.
    WORKTypes / Jean M. Kummerow, Linda K. Kirby, and Nancy J. Barger.
        p.   cm.
    ISBN 978-0-446-67217-7
    1. Psychology, Industrial. 2. Labor productivity—Psychological
aspects. 3. Personality and occupation. 4. Interpersonal
communication—Psychological aspects. 5. Myers-Briggs Type
indicators. I. Kirby, Linda K. II. Barger, Nancy J. III. Title.
HF5548.8.K85   1997
158.7—dc20   96-9245
                                                                   CIP

Cover design by Irving Freeman
Interior design by Charles Sutherland

To those who've shown me the value of work, how to work, and why to work, and who have worked alongside me, including my parents, Fred and Amy Kummerow, my spouse, John Loban, and our children, Liz and Rob Loban.

Jean Kummerow

To our children:
Mark, Matthew, and Andrew Barger
Pam and Zachary Kirby

Nancy Barger and Linda Kirby

Acknowledgments

Writing a book is a joint project with many people behind the scenes. We appreciate the help and support of:

Ruth Johnson and Jeanne Kirby for their logistical provisions of good food and a wonderful cabin in the Colorado Rockies, which made our writing venue a pleasant one.

Betsy, a terrific dog who dreams of being a coyote, who kept us company and provided pleasant diversions.

A number of readers including friends, family, colleagues, and Jean's fellow book club members for their useful comments and their different perspectives: Michelle Anderson, Paul Anderson, Ginny Brodeen, Pat Golfis, Katy Gray, Kathy Heiderich, Becky Hutchinson, Karen Kolb, Kay Kummerow, Ona Lentz, Sue Martland, Mary Melbo, Kathy Monahan-Rial, Margie Njus, and John Witek.

Diana Baroni, our Warner Books editor, who kept us on target and on schedule.

Thanks to you all!

Contents

WORK
Types

INTRODUCTION

very day, everywhere in the world, millions of us go to work. Some of us find work to be exciting, challenging, and interesting. And some of us are frustrated with our work and feel less productive than we want to be. The experts tell us that we are undergoing fundamental shifts in the way we work and in the relationships between organizations and their employees. The future of work is unclear, but it seems certain that it will be radically different. Some would say it is already radically different.

In the meantime, however, work goes on, and the normal work activities still have to be completed within the changing environment. We still find ourselves entering data into computers, filling out forms, going to meetings, solving problems, making decisions, learning new things, and getting into conflicts with colleagues or bosses. The primary effect of the changing environment right now is to add additional stress to our work lives: We must do more with less—less time, fewer people, fewer resources.

Solutions for Real Problems

This is not a book about transforming work or creating the corporate model for the year 2010. This book is not even about transforming yourself into an empowered, risk-taking, highly productive, customer-oriented entrepreneurial employee. These are all important issues, but here we're concerned about something we find more fundamental and something that will not disappear in the "new corporation": you, your work style, and how you can take who you are and use that to do your work in more satisfying ways.

This book is written for you if

- you get frustrated by the amount of time you spend in unproductive meetings;
- time management seems like an elusive concept;
- teams you're on are bogged down and unproductive;
- your good ideas fall on deaf ears;
- you want to make the most of change; or
- you can't seem to get your boss's attention.

Handling these issues is not simple, and often a variety of factors goes into solving each one. Certainly job performance is impacted by the job skills you have, but your job performance is also impacted by your personality. This book is about personality, or rather one factor of it—psychological type. Work seems to be more satisfying when it is compatible with your personality.[1]

This book takes everyday work activities and reframes them into the language of psychological type; we're adding a different perspective to the tasks you already handle. The everyday work activities we've included are those we see as common to most workers and the ones we get asked to help with most frequently. Each chapter presents common situations you might identify with from your work setting. We discuss techniques people currently use and integrate a type perspective into those techniques. We then offer descriptions, strategies, and tips based on psychological type to help you and your colleagues deal more effectively with these kinds of situations, including negotiating for what you need. We hope that using this book over a period of time will help you recognize and pay more attention to your natural style so that you can make the most of it at work.

Psychological Type

Psychological type provides tools to help you look at ways you get reenergized, how you define your work, how you make decisions, and how you structure your work and complete your tasks.

An understanding of psychological type

1. helps you understand your own work style, and provides ways to support and extend your own areas of strength to compensate for your areas of weakness;
2. leads to understanding the approaches and needs of those you work with, thus allowing you to resolve conflicts related to type;
3. gives you starting points for negotiating so that people (you and others) get what they need and can do their best work;
4. provides a way to discuss interpersonal issues that have been avoided at work. Sometimes people simply haven't known how to identify something that just "doesn't seem

right," or how to talk about it without making things worse.

If you're already familiar with psychological type, you may use the next chapter as a refresher, but feel free to skip to chapters on the issues of concern in your work life today. If you haven't been introduced to the theory of psychological type, we invite you to read the next chapter first. Reading *LIFE-Types*[2] will give you a broader introduction, and we also highly recommend that to you. You may wish to take an inventory designed to indicate your type preferences, the Myers-Briggs Type Indicator® (MBTI®) assessment tool. You may be able to take it from your organization's human resources department. Many community-college and university counselors as well as private practitioners and church professionals are also qualified to administer and interpret this tool.

Who Should Read This Book

This is a book for real people at all levels in organizations, from clerk to chief executive officer, from sole proprietor to multinational corporate employee. It deals with common everyday work requirements and interactions.

Each workday we have tasks to complete efficiently, meetings to go to, and ongoing relationships that need support and respect. We all have responsibility to make our work as productive as possible and, if we do, we can leave work each day feeling satisfied with our accomplishments.

Wherever people live, in almost every work setting—from small nonprofit organizations to global communications companies—they face these tasks daily. These tasks have no boundaries.

As consultants who work internationally, we've faced these issues around the globe and have found solutions that work. We know that people want to do well at their work, put tremendous energy into it, and take pride in their results. We think our suggestions will help.

Reading This Book

The next chapter will introduce you to, and help you identify, your type and the types of those you work with. We are not suggesting that your speculations are enough to confirm a type; taking the MBTI instrument and having it interpreted by a qualified professional is needed. When you're ready, the rest of the book helps you apply that type knowledge to your work.

Chapters 2 through 6 discuss fundamental issues in the workplace: communication and conflict, time management, meetings, leadership, and teamwork. In these chapters, we apply the basics of type (the individual preferences, various combinations of preferences, and the whole type) to help you grasp how type can aid in your understanding of these work tasks. You may wish to skip around and use these chapters for reference as needed. Chapter 7 introduces another level of type, called type dynamics, and is necessary background for Chapters 8 and 9 on change and stress. We finish the book with examples of how people have put the information to use. You may find you recognize yourself and your co-workers in the chapters ahead.

CHAPTER 1

INTRODUCTION
TO TYPE

The Office Awakens

 t's nine o'clock on Monday morning and a typical day at the office: Elizabeth, a popular employee, helps get the office jump-started by visiting with her co-workers, asking how their weekend went, telling them about hers, and filling them in on what their colleagues did. She also takes this opportunity to find out about their work plans for the day. Her laughter and the easy expression of her feelings are contagious.

Irene, a highly regarded employee, is already hard at work in another way: in her cubicle tuning out the noise around her so she can concentrate on updating the department's sched- uled events for the week on the computer. She likes to do this first thing to get everyone's week off to a good start. Also, on Friday afternoon, she'd run into a computer problem. Over the weekend, she had thought of a possible solution, and was eager to try it out to see if it worked.

6

Steve, known for his common sense, is the one the staff relies on to give a realistic appraisal of any situation. He knows what's worked well in the past and what's likely to work well in the present. He also usually knows what resources are available and who controls them.

Nathan, known as an "ideas" man, is the one the staff relies on to point out a new direction when they feel stuck. He's always reinterpreting situations and finding a new way to look at them. They can count on him to be up on the latest ideas and theories in the field and to share them enthusiastically with anyone who's interested.

Teresa, known for her clear analyses, is on the phone with a customer who has a complaint. She is asking probing questions to get to the heart of the problem. Teresa then presents alternative solutions to the customer, including the pros and cons of each to help the customer make a decision. When the customer hesitates, Teresa pushes for the solution that will be quickest and most cost-effective for the customer.

Faith, the one everyone comes to with their problems, is on the phone with another customer who has a complaint. She is encouraging the customer to talk about his real concerns. Her goal is to find a win-win solution. She is tuned in to helping the customer, and is known throughout the office as someone who deals well with upset people.

Jerry, the unofficial office efficiency expert, is engaged in his typical Monday morning routine of planning out his week. He's listing everything he needs to do, then prioritizing and ordering his list. He likes to start his projects early in order to avoid a last-minute rush and always has a contingency plan for emergencies.

Peter, known for his flexibility in changing course at a moment's notice, is also looking at the week ahead. His approach is different: He lists his major projects for the week and gets ready to start on the one he is most excited about. He trusts his resourcefulness and sense of timing to help him fulfill all his responsibilities. He continually finds new ways to approach his work to be sure it's fun.

You might recognize these people—they may even be you or the people you work with. Each represents one of the eight preferences that make up psychological type. Each is acting differently from the others, yet all are being effective and contributing to the workplace.

Every workplace includes people with very different backgrounds, personalities, perspectives, skills, and styles of interacting. And the workforce of the future will be even more diverse. Finding ways to make these differences work, rather than letting them get in the way, is essential to success for any organization and the people in it. Even if one works alone at home, there will be times when others are involved; it will be important to communicate well. Understanding differences in work styles may be critical to success.

The Myers-Briggs Type Indicator and Psychological Type

The Myers-Briggs Type Indicator (MBTI) and psychological type provide ways of understanding normal differences that occur in people's everyday behaviors. The MBTI identifies four dimensions, or key sets of preferences, that affect the way people develop and act. These are the ways that people

- get and use their energy;
- gather and take in information;
- make decisions; and
- organize their lives.

Each of these dimensions has two opposite possibilities that different people prefer, and people's preferences lead to different personality types and behavior patterns. Each opposite possibility is of equal value and each personality type can make important contributions. No preference is more valuable or better than any other.

The MBTI and psychological type are based on the idea of preferences, so it is important to understand what is meant by this word. Take a minute and clasp your hands together, noticing which thumb is on top. Then clasp them putting the other thumb on top. Most people find that one of these ways is natural, comfortable, and automatic, while the other feels awkward and requires conscious thought. We can clasp our hands both ways, but we naturally prefer one over the other. This illustrates the idea of preferences in psychological type and the MBTI. Similarly, we can and do use both sides of each of the dimensions listed above, but typically one side feels more natural, easier, and more energizing. Keep in mind that preferences and abilities are two different things: We all have the ability to clasp our hands either way, but people usually prefer one way over the other.

Coming to recognize these preferences and the ways they influence people's behavior is very helpful in understanding ourselves and enhancing our interactions with our colleagues. We'll describe each of the four underlying dimensions and their two opposite sides below. For each preference, we'll also list some common components associated with each; these behaviors come from the MBTI Step II (formerly called the MBTI Expanded Analysis Report).[1]

Ways of Getting and Directing Energy:
Extraversion (E) and Introversion (I)

People direct their energy either outward or inward and get energy from those different spheres.

Those who prefer **Extraversion** have an outward focus. In our example of Elizabeth, did you notice how she liked interacting with people and how energizing that was for her? Like most other Extraverts, Elizabeth develops her thoughts by talking them through with others. There are several ways Extraversion may show itself, and some of these are listed below.

- **Initiating:** Initiating social interactions, introducing people and linking them with one another
- **Expressive:** Enjoying the sharing of thoughts and emotions with others freely—talking a lot in an upbeat, optimistic style
- **Gregarious:** Enjoying interacting with lots of people, often joining or forming groups
- **Participative:** Wanting to communicate in person through talking and listening
- **Enthusiastic:** Being where the action is and at the center of attention
- **Sociable:** Wanting to connect with others, talking over a variety of things

Those who prefer **Introversion** have an inward focus. In our example of Irene, did you notice how she enjoys creating her own space and working on her own, and how productive that is for her? Like most other Introverts, she forms her ideas best by reflecting and thinking them through by herself. There are several ways Introversion may show itself, and some of these are listed below:

- **Receiving:** Leaving social courtesies to others, seeing them as unimportant

- **Contained:** Keeping feelings and interests to themselves, solving issues on their own

- **Intimate:** Enjoying in-depth, one-on-one relationships

- **Reflective:** Liking to communicate through reading and writing

- **Quiet:** Preferring calm and quiet spaces, staying in the background

- **Independent:** Wanting to connect with the task, not necessarily other people

You probably notice that you use behaviors from both Extraversion and Introversion in your life and work, but most people find that one of these is more natural, comfortable, and energizing—it is their "home base."

Ways of Taking In or Gathering Information: Sensing (S) and Intuition (N)

People notice and pay attention to different things.

Those who prefer **Sensing** pay attention to what is real, actual, and factual. In our example of Steve, did you notice how people relied on him to know who, what, and where? Like most other Sensing types, Steve focuses on present reality. There are several ways Sensing may show itself, and some of these are listed below.

- **Concrete:** Knowing the facts, cautious not to go beyond what is known

- **Realistic:** Using common sense and focusing on cost-effectiveness

- **Practical:** Seeking applications and making ideas real

- **Experiential:** Learning about what works from experience, relying on knowledge gained from "doing"

- **Traditional:** Respecting and relying on time-honored ways of doing things

Those who prefer **Intuition** pay attention to the big picture, the patterns and connections. In our example of Nathan, did you notice how people relied on him to provide a new way of seeing things? Like most other Intuitives, Nathan focuses on future possibilities and frequently finds the future more interesting than the present. There are several ways Intuition may show itself, and some of these are listed below.

- **Abstract:** Reading between the lines and coming up with possible meanings

- **Imaginative:** Inventing clever new ways to see and do things

- **Inferential:** Liking knowledge for its own sake, searching for and collecting ideas

- **Theoretical:** Trusting theories and discovering patterns, inventing them if none exist

- **Original:** Being drawn to anything new, desiring a strong sense of personal uniqueness

Again, you probably notice that you use behaviors from both Sensing and Intuition in your life and work, but most people find that one of these is more natural, comfortable, and energizing—it's their "home base."

Ways of Making Decisions:
Thinking (T) and Feeling (F)

People make their decisions either through objective, logical analyses (Thinking) or through applying person-centered values (Feeling).

Those who prefer **Thinking** step back from the situation and assess pros and cons from a detached perspective. Did you notice Teresa's focus on identifying and solving the problem? Like most other Thinking types, Teresa really enjoys the challenge of solving a problem—the tougher the better—and believes that applying systematic criteria will lead to the best solution. There are several ways Thinking may show itself, and some of these are listed below.

- **Logical:** Ideally, making decisions based on the pros and cons
- **Reasonable:** Demonstrating logic and clarity in actual decisions
- **Questioning:** Feeling compelled to ask a lot of questions about everything
- **Critical:** Believing it's important to point out what's wrong, to be skeptical
- **Tough:** Being convinced of the rightness of a decision, pushing it through

Those who prefer **Feeling** put themselves into a situation to empathize with the people involved and personalize it. Did you notice Faith's emphasis on discovering the customer's needs and finding ways to support the customer? Like most other

Feeling types, Faith focuses on harmony and wants all people involved to feel satisfied with the outcome and the interaction. There are several ways Feeling may show itself, and some of these are listed below.

- **Empathetic:** Ideally, making decisions by trusting one's own emotional responses
- **Compassionate:** Using one's likes and dislikes, based on personal values, in actual decisions
- **Accommodating:** Taking the position that "if it's really important to you, I'll go along with it"
- **Accepting:** Tolerating other views, attempting to find something good in all people or ideas
- **Tender:** Seeing both sides of an issue, searching for consensus

To repeat a point, you probably notice that you use behaviors from Thinking and Feeling in your life and work, but most people find that one of these is more natural, comfortable, and energizing—it's their "home base."

Organizing Our Lives:
Judging (J) and Perceiving (P)

People choose to organize their lives through plans and structures (Judging) or through spontaneity and flexibility (Perceiving).

Those who prefer **Judging** focus on identifying goals, planning how to reach them, and following through to get them completed. Did you notice that Jerry wanted to structure his time before the week started, so he could feel comfortable with starting his work? Like most other Judging types, Jerry wants closure and a sense of completion in a timely manner in everything he's involved in or responsible for. There are several ways Judging may show itself, and some of these are listed below.

- **Systematic:** Planning thoroughly for whatever might arise, having contingency plans in place
- **Planful:** Feeling it's one's duty to make long-range plans
- **Early Starting:** Beginning early to avoid the stress of last-minute rush
- **Scheduled:** Relying on routines as the most efficient and comfortable ways to get things done
- **Methodical:** Developing precise, step-by-step ways to complete immediate tasks

Those who prefer **Perceiving** focus on gathering all the information and know that, whatever the challenge, they can pull it off. Did you notice that Peter has a general sense of direction and wants to remain open to whatever may come up? Like most other Perceiving types, Peter feels comfortable in letting his schedule emerge and relies on and trusts his inner sense of timing. There are several ways Perceiving may show itself, and some of these are listed below.

- **Casual:** Enjoying surprises and going with the flow
- **Open-ended:** Wanting to keep options open, disliking unchangeable plans
- **Pressure-Prompted:** Waiting until the last minute in order to take advantage of the rush of energy that comes then

- **Spontaneous:** Disliking routines, finding different ways to do things to maintain one's interest
- **Emergent:** Trusting that what to do next will appear when it's needed

And to emphasize a very important point, you probably notice that you use behaviors from both Judging and Perceiving in your life and work, but most people find that one of these is most natural, most energizing—it is their "home base."

Psychological Type and the MBTI

The preferences and behaviors we've identified in the previous section have their origins in Swiss psychologist Carl Jung's theories about human beings. Isabel Briggs Myers and Katharine Briggs, two Americans, developed the MBTI to help people identify those preferences. They designed and tested their instrument beginning in the 1940s, and it has become the most widely used personality inventory in the world for understanding everyday behavior.

People normally develop behavior patterns consistent with their psychological type preferences. The MBTI Step II (formerly called the MBTI Expanded Analysis Report) reports additional behavior patterns that people of a particular preference tend to develop. We listed those components above, along with information about the broader preferences E, I, S, N, T, F, J, and P to which they belong.

The Sixteen Types

The four preferences combine into sixteen types, commonly reported in letter form. Each type has both strengths and weaknesses, and each can make unique contributions at work. The following are brief descriptions of each of the sixteen types, excerpted from *LIFETypes*,[2] which contains longer, more indepth portraits of each type. Most people find it helpful to personalize the type descriptions by thinking of people they know who exhibit the behaviors in the different descriptions. We are not suggesting that your speculations are enough to confirm a type; taking the instrument and having it interpreted by a qualified professional is needed. Be careful not to stereotype!

ISTJ

ISTJs are systematic, painstaking, thorough, and hardworking. They get the job done and complete it on schedule. They are serious and sincere in whatever they do. They work well within a structure, follow the hierarchy, and are particularly strong and careful in keeping track of facts and details. They are cautious, generally seeking to maintain the status quo. They are at their best getting things to the right place at the right time. They honor their commitments.

ISTP

ISTPs are realists who apply expediency and reasoning as they manage and adapt to situations. They are aware of what is going on in the environment and are able to respond quickly to the actual facts, making sure the odds of success are in their favor. They do not like to be tied down and will feel hamstrung when they must operate within tight structures and schedules. They are able to anticipate immediate, practical needs in situations and to present a logical, straightforward plan for meeting those needs. They are at their best in situations that require immediate attention.

ESTP

ESTPs are action-oriented, pragmatic, outgoing, and realistic people. In situations that require resourcefulness, they use their quickness and flexibility to find the most efficient route to accomplishing whatever needs to be done. They are lively, entertaining, and fun. They like to be where the action is and participate fully in what is happening. Characteristically, they are direct with their comments and mince no words. They are at their best in situations that require an orientation to the present and a direct, no-nonsense, pragmatic approach.

ESTJ

ESTJs are doers who roll up their sleeves, dig in, and proceed directly to get the job done. They see logic and analysis as guiding principles for their lives. They are quick to decide and set a plan of action. They marshal resources in an organized fashion, implement, and follow through. They like closure. They focus directly on tasks to accomplish and are able to anticipate the steps needed to complete an assignment. In doing so, they see what might go wrong and take the necessary preventive action. They monitor events continually and make sure that commitments, both their own and those of others, are honored and the job gets done. They are at their best in situations that have some structure to them and involve activity, not contemplation, and in which an end product is desired.

ISFJ

ISFJs are sympathetic, loyal, considerate, and conscientious. They will go to any amount of trouble, when it makes sense to them, to help those in need. ISFJs operate most comfortably in situations where the rules are well defined and where traditions are to be upheld. They focus on providing practical help and service for others and for the organizations they serve. They are often self-effacing in getting the job done, and they are willing to make necessary sacrifices, especially for their families. They are at their best quietly providing assistance and making sure things are in proper order.

ISFP

ISFPs are gentle and compassionate, open and flexible. They are considerate of others and do not force their views and opinions on them. They often focus on meeting others' needs, especially those who are less fortunate. Having a quiet, modest, self-effacing style, ISFPs avoid disagreements and seek harmony with people as well as with nature. They enjoy life's precious moments and often add a touch of beauty to the environments where they spend their time. They are at their best ensuring others' well-being.

ESFP

ESFPs are friendly, outgoing, fun loving, and naturally drawn to people. They are quite enthusiastic and exuberant, and are usually well liked by others. They are good at meeting people and helping them enjoy themselves. They are sympathetic toward people and generous with their time and money. They want to be where the action is, and they will often stir things up in their own special way. At their best, they are able to realistically meet human and situational needs in a fun and lively way.

ESFJ

ESFJs are helpful people who place a high value on harmony. Paying close attention to people's needs and wants, they work well with others to complete tasks in a timely and accurate way. ESFJs follow through on their commitments. They like closure and prefer structured, organized situations in which warmth and compassion are shown. They contribute to others by anticipating their day-to-day concerns and handling them with warmth and efficiency. ESFJs are at their best in organizing people to get a job done.

INFJ

INFJs are future oriented, and direct their insight and inspiration toward the understanding of themselves and thereby human nature. Their work mirrors their integrity, and it needs to reflect their inner ideals. Solitude and an opportunity to concentrate thoroughly on what counts most are important to them. INFJs prefer to quietly exert their influence. They have deeply felt compassion, and they desire harmony with others. INFJs understand the complexities existing within people and among them. They do not call a great deal of attention to themselves, preferring that their contributions speak for them. They are at their best concentrating on their ideas, ideals, and inspirations.

INFP

INFPs focus deeply on their values, and they devote their lives to pursuing the ideal. They often draw people together around a common purpose and work to find a place for each person within the group. They are creative, and they seek new ideas and possibilities. They quietly push for what is important to them, and they rarely give up. While they have a gentleness about them and a delightful sense of humor, they may be somewhat difficult to get to know and may be overlooked by others. They are at their best making their world more in line with their internal vision of perfection.

ENFP

ENFPs are initiators of change who are keenly perceptive of possibilities, and who energize and stimulate through their contagious enthusiasm. They prefer the start-up phase of a project or relationship, and are tireless in the pursuit of newfound interests. ENFPs are able to anticipate the needs of others and to offer them needed help and appreciation. They bring zest, joy, liveliness, and fun to all aspects of their lives. They are at their best in situations that are fluid and changing, and that allow them to express their creativity and use their charisma.

ENFJ

ENFJs are lively and enthusiastic facilitators who apply warmth and vision to helping people and meeting their needs. They are aware of people's aspirations and develop plans of action to make those aspirations into reality. They like organization and closure. They are at their best facilitating situations that require interpersonal sensitivity. ENFJs are tolerant and appreciative of others, seeking involvement with them in life's tasks. They are able communicators who are liberal in showing appreciation for others.

INTJ

INTJs are strong individualists who seek new angles or novel ways of looking at things. They enjoy coming to new understandings. They are insightful and mentally quick; however, this mental quickness may not always be outwardly apparent to others since they keep a great deal to themselves. They are very determined people who trust their vision of the possibilities, regardless of what others think. They may even be considered the most independent of all of the sixteen personality types. INTJs are at their best in quietly and firmly developing their ideas, theories, and principles.

INTP

INTPs are known for their quest for logical purity, which motivates them to examine universal truths and principles. They are constantly asking themselves and others the questions Why? and Why not? Clear and quick thinkers, they are able to focus with great intensity on their interests. They appreciate elegance and efficiency in thought processes and require them, even more so, in their own communications. They may be seen as unwilling to accept what everyone else regards as truth. While often low-key in outward appearance and approach, the INTP is "hard as nails" when challenging a truth. INTPs do not like to deal with the obvious. They are at their best in building conceptual models and developing unusual and complex ideas.

ENTP

ENTPs are known for their quest of the novel and complex. They have faith in their ability to improvise and to overcome any challenges that they face. They are highly independent, and value adaptability and innovation. They may be several steps ahead of others in encouraging and valuing change. ENTPs hate uninspired routine and resist hierarchical and bureaucratic structures that are not functional. They need freedom for action. With their entrepreneurial tendencies and broad understandings, they push against all odds to further their projects. They are at their best in changing circumstances in which they can develop conceptual models and devise strategies to effectively navigate through change.

ENTJ

ENTJs take charge quickly and deal directly with problems, especially in situations that involve confusion and inefficiency. They provide structure to the organizations to which they belong and design strategies to accomplish their personal and organizational goals. They develop broad, action-oriented plans, and supply the necessary energy and momentum to see that these plans are accomplished. ENTJs are "take charge" people who organize their own and others' external environments. They do not take no for an answer; instead, they use their resources to find a way to meet the challenge. They are at their best in using their analytical and strategic thinking.

Using Type Knowledge to Help You at Work

The general principles for using knowledge of your own type to develop your effectiveness, skills, and abilities at work are the following:

1. Recognize your natural strengths and find ways to make the maximum use of them.
2. Accept that you do not do everything equally well and identify areas where you have blind spots, make mistakes, or get into difficulty.
3. Identify tools and resources, including other people, to help you manage your weaker areas or improve your skills.

In later chapters, we give more information about type preferences and type combinations as we examine specific work tasks and roles. This material will help you with the three steps above.

Type knowledge can also help you in dealing with co-workers, bosses, or those you supervise. The general principles for using type knowledge to interact more effectively with others are the following:

1. Recognize that others have different perspectives and needs than you do. (It's a given that we're not all alike!) They also have the same right to have their approaches counted and used as you have.
2. Acknowledge that your work will be more effective if it includes others' perspectives and ideas. They can save you from serious oversights and mistakes, can help you get unstuck, and can help you develop new abilities.
3. Find ways to make constructive use of the differences.

Personalizing Type

As you read through the next chapters, you may find yourself identifying with your own type a great deal, and less so with the descriptions of other types. It's easier to apply this information if you can identify people you know of a given type. Millions of people throughout the world have taken the MBTI—perhaps some of them are your colleagues. You might have made some note of them when you read the short type descriptions.

Please keep in mind that each type can make valuable contributions in the workplace. There are no "better" or "worse" types, simply different perspectives and natural strengths. Begin by identifying as clearly as possible your own type preferences (remember, it's best to take the instrument and have it interpreted by a qualified professional). Then learn about your co-workers. Don't be surprised if some people of the same type seem to be somewhat different from one another; type is just one factor in a person's personality. And finally, begin to apply your knowledge of your psychological differences to your work.

How *Not* to Use Type at Work

Type and the MBTI are about underlying preferences and behavior patterns. A lot of other factors also influence the behaviors and skills we have developed. Type is not intended to be a box, limiting the kinds of things you or others can do. Every occupation includes all sixteen types. In addition, the MBTI does *not* measure skills or tell us how well we use a preference: Preferring Sensing does not guarantee that Sensors see the right details; preferring Intuition does not mean that all Intuitives see the appropriate big picture.

Thus, we shouldn't use knowledge of type preferences to assign people to certain jobs, to avoid certain activities, or to excuse inexcusable behavior. The best use of the MBTI is what we have outlined above: to understand ourselves and others better in order to work (together) more effectively.

CHAPTER 2

COMMUNICATION
AND CONFLICT

herever people work—in an office, a factory, or at home—there are common complaints about communication: There's too much, there's too little, it's not the right kind, or it's not between the right people. We've heard a lot of people say:

- "Nobody listens to me."
- "Nobody takes me seriously."
- "I tried to tell them . . . , but they went ahead anyway."
- "They just don't understand me."
- "If he says that one more time, I swear I'm going to. . . ."
- "They didn't tell the rest of us until. . . ."
- "If only they had asked the people who knew."

Many factors besides psychological type enter into the ways people communicate—the organizational culture and values, power relationships, the resources available, the skills people have—but type can illuminate important components and offer perspectives and skills that can help us improve.

Communication

We cannot **not** communicate. We are always communicating—whether we speak or don't speak. Communication is about what we say, how we say it, when we choose not to say something, how we listen, and when we stop listening. Type has a lot to do with each of these areas. Thus, most of the chapters in this book relate directly or indirectly to communication. Here we want to summarize some basic relationships between type preferences and communication patterns, many of which we will discuss in more detail later.

Communication Styles:
What's Type Got to Do with It?

Each of the type dimensions described in the previous chapter affects communication styles. The first preference dimension, Extraversion/Introversion, relates to people's styles in interacting and engaging in conversations. The second, Sensing/Intuition, typically influences the kinds of information people focus on when speaking, listening, or writing. The third, Thinking/Feeling, may relate most directly to the individual's decision to participate or to tune out. And the final one, Judging/Perceiving, impacts the structure and style of communications.

Extraversion (E) and Introversion (I):
Styles of Interacting and Engaging in Verbal Communication

Extraversion (E)—People with this preference usually want to know what is going on and to be included in all communications. They want opportunities to talk everything through and will develop their thoughts through interaction with others. When they are engaged and involved, they typically talk a lot, speak rapidly, build on what others are saying, and may interrupt others in their excitement. They think out loud!

Introversion (I)—People with this preference usually prefer written communication because they want to think through their own information base and ideas before "going public" with them. In verbal communication, they want to be able to reflect on what's being said and then have an opening to speak. At times, it is hard for them to find that opening. When they are engaged and involved, it doesn't necessarily show on the outside; they may give few nonverbal cues and may not express their thoughts.

MUTUAL MISINTERPRETATIONS:
"THAT ISN'T WHAT I MEANT"

We might think of the two different verbal communication styles and their misinterpretations this way:

Extraversion—Speak, listen, speak, speak, listen, speak, speak, speak—then perhaps reflect. This style may appear rude to *I*s; the rapid speaking, the interruptions, and the building on each other's ideas may seem to exclude the more deliberate style of Introverts, and not to give an opening for their contributions.

Introversion—Listen, reflect, listen, reflect, reflect, reflect—then perhaps speak. This style of thinking it through inside before speaking can be very difficult for *E*s to understand. They may interpret it as not being interested or involved, or they may assume that the Introvert is disapproving or judgmental, or worse yet, too stupid to respond.

TIPS FOR EXTRAVERTS

1. Be aware that your style can overwhelm Introverts (and other Extraverts, too!). If you see that others are not speaking, slow down a little, pause, allow silence, ask others for their thoughts, and listen. In a group, you may need to say something like, "What other ideas do you all have?" being careful not to put anyone in particular on the spot. With an individual, you might say something like, "Kara, I know you have some experience in this area. Can you give your perspective on this?"

2. Build in a new step before leaving any topic, a step that allows time in the agenda for everyone to add their input: "Does anyone else have some ideas that apply to this topic? Are we finished with this, or do we need to revisit it later?"

3. If you are feeling that someone is uninterested or tuned out when you are talking, instead of proceeding on that assumption, ask for feedback. Perhaps you can say something like this: "It would help me to know where you are on this," and then listen to what they say. They may indeed be uninterested in contributing to that topic and may say, "I have nothing further to add," or they may have something to say. You'll never know unless you ask.

TIPS FOR INTROVERTS

1. Recognize that you have a responsibility to let others know where you are and what you need. Be aware that some people may be misinterpreting your silence and drawing incorrect assumptions if you don't say what's on your mind. You might say something like, "I have some information about this, but I need a few minutes (or a few days!) to think it through and organize it so it can be helpful to us." Decide how and when you will communicate to those who need/want to know.

2. Ask that a particular topic be tabled for now and revisited before the end of the conversation or meeting, when what you have to offer may be clearer to you.

3. Be willing to give feedback to others—in a nonjudgmental way—when their interruptions or pace are causing problems for you. You might say something like, "I want to participate in this, but I'm feeling that I can't get a word in edgewise. Can we step back and find a better process?"

TIPS FOR ALL

As often as possible, and especially on important issues, provide both written communication prior to face-to-face conversations (for Introverts) and also opportunities for face-to-face discussion, questions, and expression of opinions and ideas (for Extraverts). Specifically, in meetings, that means written agendas ahead of time and opportunities in the actual meeting for discussions.

Sensing (S) and Intuition (N):
The Kind of Information Focused on in Communications

Sensing (S)—People with this preference usually want to focus on what is real and actual in the present or past: Who?

What? Where? When? They typically give and want real-life examples. When Ss are engaged and involved, they will ask a lot of specific questions to learn the details and will give a lot of relevant information and examples.

Intuition (N)—People with this preference usually want to move every communication to a bigger context, to the connections, and to wider meanings. When Ns are engaged and involved, they brainstorm, leap to other topics they see as connected, and offer different perspectives.

MUTUAL MISINTERPRETATIONS: "THAT ISN'T WHAT I MEANT"

Misinterpretations can result because each of these preferences focuses on different kinds of information.

Sensing questions and contributions may seem to Ns to be picky, to slow down the process, to be pessimistic, to show resistance to change, and to be boring and unimaginative. Ns will sometimes express it this way: "Whatever idea I have, she always shoots it down."

Intuitive questions and contributions may seem to Ss to be irrelevant and off topic, to obscure the real issues, to prolong the process, and to be unrealistic, unhelpful, and frustrating. Ss will sometimes express it this way: "He's really off the wall, so vague and impractical. I mean, we're trying to decide on a name for our new product and he's telling us Greek myths."

TIPS FOR SENSORS

1. Be aware that your helpful questions or useful details may cut off another's sharing of information or may

short-circuit another's Intuitive process or brainstorm. Ask others, "Do you want my input now, or would it be more helpful later?" If the answer is later, jot down your comments so you won't forget them.

2. Give others the context for your details and your questions: "I think this is really a good idea, and I'd like to help make it work. Here are some of the pieces I may be able to help with: Who's going to be responsible for . . ." Or "I'm concerned about . . . and its potential impact on your idea."

3. Ask others to help you with some of the context or wider meanings of your own ideas. For example, when you present an idea or plan, say something like, "I've tried to think through how this might work. I wonder if some of you might have ideas about how this fits with what other departments in the company are doing."

TIPS FOR INTUITIVES

1. Recognize that others may need to "try out" your ideas by fleshing out the realities or by relating them to their experience. Their "picky" comments may actually be their effort to ground your vision or gain insight into their reality so they can consider and support it.

2. Be aware that your insights, broader perspectives, and natural "leaps" may simply confuse others or seem like distractions. Try to provide the link to the present problem or discussion topic that will allow them to use your insight: "Ralph, your plan for reorganizing the flow of reports identifies some problem areas. I have a thought about another way to look at potential solutions that may fit better with the changes going on throughout our company."

3. Try to identify specific times for brainstorming and for evaluating ideas, perhaps even putting those times on the agenda. After generating some ideas, make time to list, for example, "What would make this idea work" and then "What would get in the way." In other words, find ways to get value from the Sensing perspective, which may be more realistic and practical than yours.

TIPS FOR ALL

Both types of information are crucial for the success of organizations, departments, teams, and individuals. Be sure to find ways to value and give time to both kinds in every communication—written or oral (for some helpful suggestions on doing this, see Chapter 5 and Chapter 6).

Thinking (T) and Feeling (F): Deciding to Participate, to Be Engaged in the Communication Process

Thinkers (T)—People with this preference want a logical structure and clarity in communication, and for communications to focus on the work. *T*s will tune out and stop participating when there's too much time spent on things that seem irrelevant to them such as personal emotions, or when others seem to "ramble" and don't appear to have any points to make.

Feelers (F)—People with this preference want communications to have a personal connection to them, to people, or to their values and interests. *F*s will tune out by shifting their attention away from the topic when the communication is too detached, when there's interpersonal tension, when they don't like the person talking, or when impacts on people are not being considered.

MUTUAL MISINTERPRETATIONS: "THAT ISN'T WHAT I MEANT"

Given such different focuses, misunderstandings can occur and may lead to discounting the communication of others.

The **Thinking (T)** focus on task, problem, and logic may be interpreted by Feelers as critical, negative, and cold. They may see *T*s as not caring about people, not concerned with what's really important to the F.

The **Feeling (F)** focus on relationships and people may be interpreted by Thinkers as irrelevant, fluffy, not tough enough, and too personal. They may be uncomfortable with F intensity or expression of emotions and may see F questions and focus as "bogging down" the decision-making process.

TIPS FOR THINKING TYPES

1. Recognize that personal connection and individual acknowledgment are essential for Feeling types to commit their energy fully to communication. This is not "fluff" or wasted time, but instead part of making the process of communication work.
2. Be aware that your logical, analytical, dissecting approach may obscure your genuine concerns about the impact on people. Instead of assuming that others will know this, be sure to express that concern clearly as one important component in your thinking.
3. Realize that what you might experience as a lively difference of opinion or a healthy exchange of viewpoints may feel like conflict to Feeling types. They may be hesitant to offer their viewpoint or may be distracted by the

tension they are experiencing (often triggered from non-verbal communication such as voice tone) or be fearful of the consequences if they enter the dialogue. Especially if others are quiet, you may need to ask how the process is working for them.

TIPS FOR FEELING TYPES

1. Recognize that logical structure and clarity are important for Thinking types to be able to engage in communication. This is not necessarily cold or impersonal, but instead is part of allowing them to participate fully in the communication process.

2. Be aware that your inclusive, relationship-oriented approach may be seen as obscuring your commitment to planning and completing tasks. Instead of assuming that others know that, be sure to express it clearly as an important goal for you.

3. Realize that you need to take responsibility for letting others know when the process of the communication is not working for you. You may need to say something like, "I'm aware of a lot of tension and anger here, and it's getting in the way of my focusing on the task. Can we spend some time looking at the process we're using?"

TIPS FOR ALL

Both focuses (task for *T*s and people for *F*s) are important for good communication and both are necessary for engaging everyone in communication. It's important to find ways to include both Thinking and Feeling needs in written and verbal communications. (Chapter 5 has more specific suggestions for doing this.)

Judging (J) and Perceiving (P): The Style of the Conversation—Structure or Flow?

Judging (J)—People with this preference usually want written and verbal communication to be goal oriented and to the point. They prefer a clear structure: Introduce the topic, finish the topic, and move on to the next point. For *J*s, communications need to have a beginning, a short middle, and an end. They say, "Okay, we're done with that, what's next?"

Perceiving (P)—People with this preference usually want to get on the conversational wave and go with it, and their written communications often demonstrate the same style: They will veer off into interesting areas or digressions, suggest additional information that would be helpful, and leave the topic open. For *P*s, the information and exploration is more important than the conclusion. Communications need to have a beginning, a long middle, and an end that comes when they are ready. They say, "That's interesting; have you thought about . . . ?"

MUTUAL MISINTERPRETATIONS: "THAT ISN'T WHAT I MEANT"

These differences can lead to negative experiences, and either may be critical of the other.

The goal-orientation, structuring, and closure of **Judging (J)** communications may make *P*s feel pushed, pressured, and controlled. They may say, "What's the point of talking about it—you've already decided." Perceiving types can become quite rebellious in this environment.

The exploration, information-seeking, and openness of **Perceiving (P)** communications may seem to *J*s to be directionless, frustrating, and irresponsible. They may ask, "Look, are we going to make a decision and move on here, or are we just going to go around in circles?"

TIPS FOR JUDGING TYPES

1. Recognize that your structuring may feel restrictive and confining to Perceiving types and that your suggestions for solutions may sound like you've already made a decision. Limit the structure you provide to the essentials: Define how you see the problem (and identify it as yours, not "This *is* the problem"), list some of the options you see, invite others' ideas and information, and give a *general* time frame for deciding.

2. Be aware that your style of communication may sometimes close things off before additional facts or all the relevant information has been gathered. Try to distinguish between when a decision really has to be made now and when your push to a decision is coming out of your desire for closure. You may try "asking" instead of "pushing." Practice leaving decisions open that can be left open.

3. Agree on general time parameters and leave others to establish their own processes within those—do not insist that others come up with structures in the way that you do ("I want a memo tomorrow outlining the steps you are going to take"), but instead hold them to the final result.

Recognize that structures you find comfortable and necessary may be rigid and unnecessary for others.

TIPS FOR PERCEIVING TYPES

1. Recognize that your exploration style may feel like meandering and wasting time to Judging types, and ultimately you may lose your listener. Convey your general time frame to them: "I'd like us to discuss and agree on what the problem actually is first, then identify some of the kinds of information that would be helpful and divide up responsibility for gathering it. I'm hopeful we'll be ready to make a decision on this by next Friday."

2. Be aware that your communication style may sometimes keep things open too long and that sometimes decisions have to be made with incomplete information. Try to distinguish decisions where the consequences of waiting will be more negative than the consequences of proceeding without perfect information. Practice making decisions before you are entirely comfortable.

3. Explain to others that you take deadlines very seriously and will meet real ones responsibly. Acknowledge that others may not be comfortable with the way you get to that deadline, but ask them to evaluate you by the final result, not the process they see.

TIPS FOR ALL

Much of the advice on memo writing and meeting communication supports the Judging style of communicating, and organizational cultures usually see this as "the right way." It's important to include what Judging types need, but it's also important not to lose the potential contributions of Perceiving types in bringing in new information. Invite additional written and verbal communications wherever possible.

Improving Your Communication Skills

Communication is a two-way street; it is an exchange. Listening is as important a component as speaking. We are all familiar with the following situations:

- Ongoing groups or relationships where people have developed scripts—routinized ways of interacting—that do not really involve "communication." One of the most familiar of these is the teenager-parent interaction, where each knows exactly what the other will say and tunes out whenever the other starts on his or her routine.
- Employees scanning and discarding memos from the supervisor who harps on the same issues in the same way.
- Tuning out in meetings when people start on their familiar "shtick."
- "Conversations" where people are simply waiting for the other to pause so that they can say what they want to say.

These are all situations that theoretically involve communication but where there is little actual dialogue occurring.

Using the theory of type provides perspectives and suggestions that can help people give information to others more effectively—in ways that will allow them to tune in rather than turn off. This information can also help people listen and receive information from others more openly.

To examine these issues, we will look at the two middle letters of each type, referred to as function pairs, which indicate people's preferred ways of taking in and giving information (Sensing or Intuition) and preferred ways of making decisions (Thinking or Feeling). These two middle-letter combinations (Sensing-Thinking or ST, Sensing-Feeling or SF, Intuition-Feeling or NF, Intuition-Thinking or NT) influence the individual's typical desired goal in communication, may indicate what others hear, and can help identify some strategies for modifying communication and for listening more openly.

Sensing and Thinking (ISTJ, ISTP, ESTP, ESTJ)

GOAL OF COMMUNICATION

For *ST*s, the goal of communicating is to get to the bottom line, to be efficient, and not to waste time. They want to get the job done.

WHAT OTHERS MAY HEAR—POSSIBLE MISINTERPRETATIONS

When *ST*s communicate in this fashion, others may not recognize or understand the motivation, but instead may hear, experience, and interpret the ST communication as:

- blunt
- rude
- giving limited information
- giving orders
- being noncollaborative—not inviting ideas or participation
- impersonal and cold—ignoring personal relationships

How Others Can Listen More Fully
and Openly to *ST*s

1. Remember *ST*s' motivation: to solve problems quickly and efficiently. This can help you not to take *ST*s' manner personally and not to take offense at their abruptness. When you can listen more openly, you may find the ST type of communication providing solutions and structure that you and others need.
2. Ask the ST for what you need clearly, up front, and directly—for more time, more information, more explanation, more inclusion. You need to say, "Wait a minute, I need more . . . before I can go on."
3. If you have a good idea, or disagree with them and can't find a way to get your perspective in, here's a suggestion that works with many *ST*s: Acknowledge that their solution would work well, and then say you have a suggestion to improve it. You might say, "I think that would work well; I think it might be even better if we. . . ."

What *ST*s Can Do to "Soften the Blow"
(To Get Their Message Across)

1. Recognize the impact of your style on others and modify it so you can achieve your goals. This is not a waste of time or less efficient—if you can avoid offending others, your plans will be more efficiently executed in the long run. For example, acknowledge others in your verbal communications. Use the other person's name, listen to their comments, and say, "That's a good point" or "That's an interesting question."
2. Invite input from others in written and verbal communication. Before you move to the bottom line, make sure others are on board by asking for their perspective:

"What do you think I've missed here?" "Are there other ways we might approach this?"

3. On important issues—ones that will seriously affect people or the organization—state the problem and the goal, but ask for everyone's solutions. (Yours will become one option to be considered along with a number of others.)

Effective ST communication: Remember, including others improves the bottom line.

Sensing and Feeling (ISFJ, ISFP, ESFP, ESFJ)

GOAL OF COMMUNICATION

For *SF*s, the goal of communicating is to be personal, respectful, and inclusive of others to help people important to them get what they need.

WHAT OTHERS MAY HEAR—POSSIBLE MISINTERPRETATIONS

When *SF*s communicate in this fashion, others may not recognize or understand the motivation, but instead may hear, experience, and interpret the SF communication as:

• too personal, even intrusive
• ignoring problems, avoiding everything even potentially negative
• phony—too sweet and nice, even syrupy
• ignoring larger issues, especially issues of strategy
• superficial
• overly compliant with authority

How Others Can Listen More Fully

1. Remember *SF*s' motivation: to form warm, personal relationships that will facilitate the work and create a harmonious environment for everyone. When you need them to modify their style it will help you personally to do your job better. In other words, appeal to their primary goal by telling them how they can assist you.

2. Ask for what you need gently and with acknowledgment of them personally: "I appreciate the way you look for the best in everyone—your support means a lot to all of us. But we really need to solve this problem, and that requires us to identify it clearly. Can you help us with that?"

3. Be prepared to help them move to the task, after giving some time for the personal connections.

What *SF*s Can Do to Control the Caretaking (To Be Heard and Still Be Helpful)

1. Be aware that others may see personal details and caretaking as distractions from the task and may want or need to have more distance in their relationships with you. Realize that this comes from their natural style and is not an indication that they don't like you or that they are cold and uncaring. Practice limiting the number of personal details in your communications to others at work.

2. When you are having difficulty with a colleague or supervisor, think of your goals and rehearse a kind way to tell the truth. Think of it as improving your relationship, not as being negative.

3. Recognize that differences and disagreements between people are not always negative. Sometimes the tension

and discussions (which you may hear as arguments) can move people ahead in important ways. Focus on helping people clarify their views and find mutually satisfactory solutions, rather than trying to gloss over or deny the differences.

Effective SF communication: Remember, achieving work goals can increase harmony.

Intuition and Feeling (INFJ, INFP, ENFP, ENFJ)

GOAL OF COMMUNICATION

For *NF*s, the goal of communicating is to engage your attention, energy, and commitment to their ideas and beliefs. They may use analogies, metaphors, and stories from their personal experience to illustrate their points.

WHAT OTHERS MAY HEAR—POSSIBLE MISINTERPRETATIONS

When *NF*s communicate in this fashion, others may not recognize or understand the motivation, but instead may hear, experience, and interpret the NF communication as:

- rambling
- vague
- unclear
- overly optimistic and idealistic
- overly personal
- irrelevant to the task at hand
- too intense

How Others Can Listen More Fully

1. Remember *NF*s' motivation: to get you committed or involved in their ideas and beliefs in the interest of making things better for the whole world, for humankind.
2. Appreciate their ideas and values, and *then* ask for specifics: "That's interesting; you've painted a wonderful picture. How would we do that?" or "What would it look like if we did that?"
3. Tell them that a particular analogy or story was helpful, but ask if they could now summarize their idea so you can make sure you fully understand it.

What *NF*s Can Do to "Get Real" (To Be Heard and Have Their Ideas Respected)

1. Realize the impact of your style on other people and recognize that you may need to modify it to achieve your goals. Analogies, metaphors, and stories do not communicate to everyone, or they may communicate different things to different people. In your own mind, focus on achieving your goal, not on gaining approval for your style of presentation.
2. Present your ideas in a more focused and clear way: Give a brief introduction ("Here's what I'm going to tell you about" or "The problem I'm addressing is . . ."), describe your idea or vision, then conclude with a brief summary ("So here are the important points in what I've said").
3. Limit the number and length of analogies or stories you use, and conclude each one by stating the point(s) you hope the story has conveyed.
4. See questions from others as helping give substance to your ideas rather than as criticism.

Effective NF communication: Remember, realistic data will improve your idea.

Intuition and Thinking (INTJ, INTP, ENTP, ENTJ)

GOAL OF COMMUNICATION

For *NT*s, the goal of communicating is to convey their interesting, complex perspective to others. Their unspoken message is, "Listen carefully, I have some interesting information for you."

WHAT OTHERS MAY HEAR—POSSIBLE MISINTERPRETATIONS

When *NT*s communicate in this fashion, others may not recognize or understand the motivation, but instead may hear, experience, and interpret the NT communication as:

- lecturing
- arrogant and pompous
- overly complex and theoretical
- removed from the "real" world
- impersonal, detached, and cold
- exclusive or combative—putting down others' perspectives

HOW OTHERS CAN LISTEN MORE FULLY

1. Remember *NT*s' motivation: to provide understanding of complex and important issues. They will most likely contribute a model and clear points that can help you expand your perspective and knowledge on the topic.
2. Recognize that they want to deliver a whole concept.

They will be able to respond to your questions or critiques after that, but may not acknowledge you until they are done. You may be able to get response to a question earlier by introducing it this way: "I need clarification on this point before we go on."

3. Respect the explanation and model they have presented, and ask for specific information: "Your analysis is insightful; how does this relate to my work?" or "What would it look like if we did that?"

WHAT *NT*s CAN DO TO "COME DOWN OFF THEIR HIGH HORSE" (TO INVITE OTHERS TO HEAR THEM)

1. Make a personal connection—explain how your ideas relate to people's current experience or why you pursued this question: "This whole idea of collapsing departments and reorganizing by functions has been keeping me awake nights. I finally figured some things out that help me, and I'd like to see what you think about them."

2. Communicate the essential points and then invite questions and ideas from others (work out the complexity ahead of time—everyone else doesn't need to hear all the side routes, interesting possibilities you considered, differing models that you tried and rejected).

3. Remember that others will have valid ideas and relevant information, and that their input may help you improve your understanding of the issue and can especially help in implementing a model of your plan.

Effective NT communication: Remember, the most elegant theory won't work unless people "get it."

Using This Information

In applying type knowledge to improve your communication skills when dealing with others, try to implement the following:

1. Recognize your own natural style and the impact it may have on others—both positive and negative.
2. Work to modify your natural style so that others fully understand your message instead of getting hung up on your method.
3. Don't feel you have to do this alone. Ask others for information about the impact of your communication, for suggestions about what would make your communication more effective for them, and for feedback on your attempts to modify your style.

When applying type to improve your ability to hear others and make use of their communications, try to implement the following:

1. Remember their positive motivation—what they potentially have to contribute to your work.
2. Take responsibility for finding ways to get the kind of communication you need—how to ask questions of a particular person without making him or her feel defensive, how to offer input and alternative suggestions in a positive way, etc.

Additional Contributions of Type to Communication

You will find additional communication ideas and tips throughout this book, specifically in Chapter 3, Chapter 4,

Chapter 5, Chapter 6, and Chapter 8. However, in this section we want to mention briefly some of the additional ways that knowledge of psychological type has helped people improve their communication, particularly in understanding the pacing of communication.

Pacing

Pacing—the rate at which information is conveyed and communication takes place—is an important type-related difference among people and a frequent source of frustration. The following summary of typical pacing needs may help reduce the frustration:

- **Extraversion-Introversion**

  Extraverts (E) typically give information quickly and want to receive it quickly. They like conversations, meetings, and communications to be fast paced.

  Introverts (I) typically want a somewhat slower pace in verbal information exchanges—time for their reflection process and a space for their observations.

- **Sensing and Thinking (ST)** types base their pacing on what it takes to get things done; their pacing can have a kind of steamroller effect on others.

- **Sensing and Feeling (SF)** types base their pacing on others around them; their desire to include everyone can seem unnecessarily slow to others.

- **Intuition and Feeling (NF)** types base their pacing on communicating their ideas with power and persuasiveness; their pacing may frustrate others who want to get to the specifics and realities.

- **Intuition and Thinking (NT)** types base their pacing on their own ideas and explanatory patterns; their desire to give the complete, complex picture as a whole may make others feel impatient.

- **Judging-Perceiving**

    Judging (J) types typically want a clear, structured, and fairly quick pace: "We'll spend five minutes discussing the problem and getting everyone's input, then we'll vote."

    Perceiving (P) types may not share a clear preference for speed or slowness, but they will typically want flexibility and room for adjustments, which does slow down decision-making.

Where all the preferences are different, the differences in pacing can lead to total communication breakdown. ISFJs, for example, can experience ENTP communication as totally meaningless: "She flits from idea to idea, talks so fast, never gives any specifics. I don't even know what she's talking about most of the time." ENTPs may experience ISFJ communication as ponderous and inconsequential: "He's always so 'nicey-nice'—asks everyone about personal information that's really none of his business. And then he has to discuss everything in complete detail. Sometimes I think I'll scream if he doesn't just move ahead and get the business done."

Sharing a number of type preferences—even all four— does not insure good communication

Two INTPs who have developed different or contradictory explanatory systems can get locked into communication conflicts: They may listen only from within their own model and fail to hear the other's contribution genuinely.

Two ENFPs may have very different ideas about how to meet the needs of the people in the organization, be totally convinced of the importance and value of their own idea, and not hear the value in the other's approach.

Two ESTJs can have very different plans for achieving a goal efficiently and may plow ahead without talking to each other. The other's implementation of their plan can then seem obstructive and inefficient.

Two ISFJs can have very different information about what the people around them need and find it quite difficult to reconcile their different perceptions.

Good communication requires *more* than understanding another's style of communicating. Mutual trust, openness to others' ideas and information, appreciation for the power of collaborative work, and a drive to *hear* others that is as great as the desire to be *heard* all contribute to good communication.

General Tips and Strategies for Using Type-Preference Knowledge to Improve Communications

These basic differences in verbal and written communication styles can add to our knowledge about ourselves: "Oh, I guess I do interrupt people a lot" (E) or "Oh, I am pretty quiet" (I). Being more aware of one's own normal communication style through type is one step in the direction of increasing the chances that one's communication will be effective—that is, that people will listen to or read, will hear, and will understand the message.

The following are general strategies that each individual can use in applying this information:

1. Know the kind of information you want, the process that works best for you, and be willing to ask for it.
2. Recognize that others will likely want different kinds of information and processes, that they have a right to get

the kind they want, and be willing to modify your style to accommodate their needs.

Type can provide a tool for recognizing and negotiating different communication styles. Using this information can add balance to the communication process, as well as helping avoid the frustration of communications that do not meet your and others' needs.

Conflict Resolution

Conflict is also a reality of work; it is a part of work. It can't be avoided, but it can be managed. Often conflict develops as a result of breakdowns in communication. It is difficult to talk about either communication or conflict without also discussing the other: Communication can cause conflict, it's a way to express conflict, and it's a way to resolve or to perpetuate and fuel it. Likewise, conflict can interfere with communication—short-circuit it, change its style, influence the way we listen, and limit what we hear.

What most people want to know about conflict is, "How can I avoid it?" Or, if it's already here, "How can I fix it?" A better question may be, "How can I manage it?" Not all conflicts can be resolved (at times there really are two incompatible goals), but all can be managed. It is helpful to identify a conflict as early as possible, so that you can begin managing it. Psychological type may be one tool to use to identify what the conflict is.

Conflicts typically have two elements: the issue (*what* is in contention) and the relationship (between the people involved). Both are important, but one may be emphasized more than another in part based on psychological type.

Type and Conflict

Psychological type suggests that people will have different views of what's important, and that may lead to conflict in and of itself.[1] Thinking types typically focus more on the issues to be resolved, whereas Feeling types typically focus more on maintaining the relationships with the people involved. There are some conflicts in which the issues are more important (e.g., safety), and some in which the relationships are more important (e.g., partnerships). There is no one best way to resolve every conflict.

We also know that type can influence the timing of dealing with a conflict.[2] Often Extraverts want to talk about a problem (now), and Introverts prefer to withdraw from it and think it over. Respecting one another's needs to think through and talk through conflict (or to compromise and do both) may be helpful.

Steps for dealing with conflict using psychological type are closely related to the kinds of information included in improving communication. And the perspectives come out of Isabel Myers's expression of the potential value of psychological type: the ability to use differences constructively. Here are some helpful tips:

1. Recognize and understand your own perspective, with its strengths *and* its limitations.
2. Listen to and try to understand the other person within his or her own framework and motivation instead of attributing motive from your viewpoint.
3. Recognize the value of the other's goal and the potential contributions of the other outlook.
4. Ask questions to develop your understanding of the other's position and perspective.

5. Seek a solution that incorporates both people's goals, that meets the essential needs of both.

Throughout the book, you'll learn even more about what the theory of type has to say about those different perspectives, viewpoints, and outlooks. There are no magic solutions to conflicts; solving them requires acknowledging that they exist and a willingness to bring them into the open. It requires a dual focus: on the task we need to accomplish *and* on the relationships/ process involved in working toward our goal.

CHAPTER 3

TIME
MANAGEMENT

Time Management in Action

 udith (INTJ) is given the assignment to develop a
written report recommending a significant restructuring of a large department. Laura (INTP) will
work with her. The staff has been discussing this
off and on for some weeks, and they feel that the
time has arrived to put the ideas on paper, devise a plan for
implementing, and move ahead. Judith and Laura agree that
they can complete their written recommendations in two
weeks.

They have their preliminary meeting on Monday and Judith
says, "I have a pretty good idea of what we need to do; how
about if we get the general picture down on paper and then divide up the pieces to flesh them out." She begins writing due
dates in her Day-Timer and starts a "to do" list.

Laura says, "You know, since we started talking about this
in the department, I've noticed some very interesting books on

"*reengineering*" *corporations. I think they've got some interesting ways of approaching these questions that can help us think about possibilities and also give us some logic and support for what we recommend.*"

Judith: "Well, I think we basically know what we need to recommend, but if you want to spend some time putting a few ideas together first, that would be fine with me. Can you write up some of the ideas and put them in a rough outline?"

Laura: "Sure, I can do that. Actually, it will be kind of fun. I've been wanting to get into this stuff."

Tuesday and Wednesday, Judith notices that Laura has more and more books piled on her desk, with more and more bookmarks and Post-it notes in them. At various times, she notices Laura animatedly explaining things to various people. From what she overhears, Laura is telling people about someone's theories, and reading quotes from various books. She does not see Laura writing at her computer.

By Thursday, Judith is getting nervous. She says to Laura, "How are you coming on that outline? Let me see your preliminary work, so we can see if we're thinking along the same lines."

Laura has nothing on paper. She has noticed Judith watching her, looking over her shoulder the last few days, and resents it. She's into exploration, having a good time with these stimulating theories, seeing exciting connections between the ideas of different writers, waiting for things to become clearer in her mind. Judith's "checking up" has annoyed her, made her feel pushed, and, she feels, interfered with her processing of ideas. She says, "I heard yesterday about an excellent book that's just out and really pulls all this stuff together. I called and it's not in the library yet, but then I called the publisher and they're sending it to me Express Mail. I should get it by tomorrow and then this weekend I'll pull it all together."

Judith feels totally let down. It appears to her that this will be another time when someone fails to follow through, when, if the job is to be done right and on time, she will have to do it herself. She walks away without a word, goes into her office, and writes out the outline she already had in her mind on Monday. Friday morning, she gives it to Laura and says, "Here, why don't you work from this. Put in the stuff you've been reading and run off a couple of copies and we'll be ready for our Monday meeting."

Laura is incensed. She thinks: If Judith was going to do it herself, why did she agree to work with me? She had already decided what the plan should be and didn't want any additional information. People are coming up with a lot of new, interesting ideas about structuring organizations, and she doesn't care about any of them. I might as well not be a part of this, and I really don't want to because I'm sure her plan won't work—it doesn't take into account any of what's going on now or what's needed in the future. She can do it herself.

What would you have done differently if you were Judith?

What would you have done differently if you were Laura?

What's Your Time-Management Style?

Here are some questions to consider when thinking about the ways you manage your time:

How much lead time do you want when working on a project?

How much detail do you want/need about your assignment?

How much contact with people do you prefer?

What kind of ongoing support do you want?

Do you want structure to do creative thinking and work?

Do you find structure stultifying or getting in the way of working most effectively?

Time Management Defined

The goal of time management is to structure your environment and your activities so you can work most effectively and efficiently. There are many workshops on how to manage your time effectively, books with time-management plans, and products on the topic that "will change your life."

These workshops, books, and products generally see managing time as creating structures and time frames and fitting ourselves into them: a filing system for documents, a system for making and using prioritized lists, half-hour schedules for every day. This is appropriate for those who prefer Judging, especially those who prefer Sensing and Judging. They naturally create structures and time frames, feel supported once those are in place and working, and can be effective and efficient using those structures.

For those who prefer Perceiving, especially with Intuition, structures and time frames feel restrictive and don't work well. How often have you seen "poorly organized" people "turn over a new leaf," buy a Day-Timer or planner, and spend incredible energy and time putting in information about everything—what they will be doing every fifteen minutes, and on and on? Typically, a month or six weeks down the road, they have stopped using the planner, stopped putting in data, and feel guilty and/or defeated.

Key time-management activities and the preferences that they seem to typically "favor" include:

Key Activities[1]	Associated Type Preferences
Prioritizing and handling tasks	Thinking and Judging
Reducing excessive interruptions	Introversion
Responding to phone calls and written requests	Judging

Processing paperwork efficiently	Sensing and Judging
Improving documentation	Sensing and Judging
Organizing an effective filing system	Sensing and Judging
Handling paperwork by organizing your desk	Sensing and Judging

Typical time-management systems prescribe ways in which we are to do these things. These techniques seem to emphasize working in our Introverted, Sensing, Thinking, and Judging modes:

- We're to have concentrated time in which we minimize interruptions (Introversion).
- We're supposed to note the relevant details and get those done quickly (Sensing).
- We're to prioritize our tasks logically (Thinking).
- We're to structure and organize our work continually (Judging).

Unfortunately, these systems may suggest solutions that are not as helpful to those with different preferred styles.

Type and Time Management

What a type perspective adds to the idea of time management is the recognition that, to manage our time most effectively, we need first to understand our own preferred style and to recognize the elements we need to do our own best, most efficient work. The following are some suggestions for better understanding and making use of your natural skills in managing time and for interacting with others whose natural approaches may be different. Remember that people are generally more effective and efficient when they work out ways to use their own natural strengths and balance their weaknesses.

Extraversion (E) — Introversion (I)

Both can be effective, can get jobs accomplished in timely ways, but the process will look quite different. Typically, Extraverts will spend time talking and interacting with others as part of their thinking and work, while Introverts will spend more time in reflection, thinking things through by themselves.

EXTRAVERSION

Strengths:

- take action on items—move quickly through tasks
- like to have several things going on and to juggle multiple tasks
- are not thrown by interruptions—in fact, will usually welcome some

Potential problems:

- can be pulled off track by external events—easily distracted by what's just come up
- get caught up in conversations not pertinent to task
- respond to the immediate situation—not always a timely way to deal with overall plans
- answer all phone calls—which can pull them off track

Tips

For Extraverts . . .

- Recognize that you will be most energized and effective when you have frequent interactions with others, and build time into your day to interact with people and to be active (move around).

- Recognize also the need for occasionally withdrawing from others to focus on recording your thoughts and ideas or to focus quietly on your tasks. Of course, you can also use your Extraverted strengths there: If, for example, you need to write a report, consider talking out your thoughts on tape to help you get started, before you begin writing.

For those working with Extraverts . . .

- Recognize that their walking around and interacting is part of their work and important to the most effective management of their time.

- Communicate clearly where the Extraverted needs of others step on your toes—such as interfering with your own need for privacy and uninterrupted time.

INTROVERSION

Strengths:

- concentrate and focus so are less easily distracted
- complete a task before going on to something else (unless they're bored with the task!)
- reflect on time and requirements—take time out to get things in perspective

- can work effectively by themselves, whatever is going on around them
- communicate well in writing

Potential problems:

- not picking up new priorities that have shifted due to external events happening in the workplace or elsewhere
- not paying attention to new information from others
- focusing on their own priorities—may ignore priorities and needs of others

Tips

For Introverts . . .

- Recognize the need for your own space and uninterrupted time. Communicate these needs to others and develop working agreements with colleagues to honor your needs. For example, you may find it most productive to handle phone calls at certain times of the day, letting a message machine pick them up the rest of the time (of course, it's crucial to return the calls when you say you will, even if telephones are not the instrument of choice for *I*s!).
- Recognize that others need access to you and be sure to include times during the day when you are available for unstructured conversations, "chatting," and other personal interactions. These can also be times when you consciously gather information from others about what's important to them.

For those working with Introverts . . .

- Recognize and support the needs of Introverts for privacy and blocks of uninterrupted time in order to be most effective.
- Communicate clearly your own needs for interaction and information, as well as the information you have that may be helpful to them.

Sensing (S) — Intuition (N)

For Sensing types, time is real, measurable, and finite. For Intuitive types, time is a concept or framework, and is malleable or expandable. Sensing types (especially Sensing and Judging types) like to manage their time by using tools and systems that others have found helpful, refining and adapting them to their own setting. Intuitive types (especially Intuitive and Perceiving types) often try prescribed systems, but typically find they can't/don't stick with them—the structure is just too routine and confining.

SENSING

Strengths:

- keep track of essential details—seldom let things "fall through the cracks"
- pay attention to the parts or steps involved
- have a structured way for handling time and details, and consistently use the structure
- use experience to predict time required—realistic about how much time something will take

Potential problems:

- may get caught up in the wrong details since they may not have stepped back to look at the big picture and put what they are doing into the overall framework
- may stick with steps even though they don't make sense and actually waste time
- may stick with an established system even when it's no longer working
- may ignore complexity or connections that are important and that could shorten or modify a task

Tips

For Sensors . . .

- Check out time-management systems people have designed such as computer software, work-flow programs, or calendars to find one that fits for you and adapt it to your needs. Don't be afraid to throw out pieces that don't fit your circumstances, and be careful not to let the system take over—keep focused on what you need the system to do for you. In other words, make sure your focus is on completing tasks and achieving an outcome, not just on working the system "properly."
- Step back regularly to assess whether the system is still working for you, make adjustments where it is not, or even find a new system that will work better.
- Recognize that others may not feel comfortable using your system or one like it, yet can be productive in their own way—don't try to impose your system on others.
- Step back occasionally to insure that you are putting your energies into the most important priorities, not just going

through the sequence of tasks doggedly. An Intuitive may be able to help you with this.

For those working with Sensors . . .

- Remember that Sensing types see time more concretely. For example, "We need to work on this now" may mean to a Sensor that we need to do it immediately; while for an Intuitive it may mean "this week." *Be sure to clarify the meaning of words related to time.*

- Recognize their need to see pieces, clarify tasks, and structure them. If you say, "Write a report for the staff meeting on . . . ," clarify how long or detailed you want it to be, what is to be included, what you expect the final product to look like (how many pages, how many copies, what format, etc.), or point out a prototype from your files. This will save time for everyone in the long run!

- Support the questions asked by Sensing types to clarify tasks. They can help you to become clearer about what you want, as well as insure that the task will be done in the way you envisioned.

INTUITION

Strengths:

- see time as expandable
- believe all things are possible
- see connections between tasks and ways to combine tasks
- can handle multiple tasks

Potential problems:

- are often unrealistic about time required to complete tasks
- can get so caught up in complexity that they miss the basics, the simple way of getting it done, and the lessons of experience
- find it difficult to use someone else's structures
- want to do tasks a new way each time—may have difficulty staying interested and energetic about routines or repetitious activities

Tips

For Intuitives . . .

- Don't be surprised if standard time-management recommendations and systems don't work for you, and don't blame yourself. If you find yourself trying one and abandoning it in a few weeks, understand that it was not your best way of organizing your time.
- Reflect on what you can extrapolate from others' systems—find creative ways that work for you to organize your papers, phone calls, etc. For example, set aside a bag of supplies you always need, use color coding for folders, and put reminder notes in visible places, such as the door frame, for something you need to remember to take with you. Intuitives need to develop their own loose systems (separate boxes for materials related to each project, for example) and to include the option of breaking their own rules and changing their system regularly. (The Intuitive authors have found that using an alphabetical or numbering system can be helpful at times and should not be re-

jected out of hand; the Sensing author had used those systems without question for years.)

- Ask a Sensing type for help in sorting, filing, and organizing. One Intuitive type asked her Sensing colleague to help sort the mail that had piled up. The Sensing type found it enjoyable and, within a short time, a job that the N had been putting off for weeks was completed.

- Remember that systems do work for some people, and if you are part of someone's system, be prepared to give them the information they need to make their system work. For example, if someone else prefers to develop a detailed plan for their next week's work, be prepared to set firm meeting times with them for the week ahead, even if that's not important to you.

For those who work with Intuitives . . .

- Recognize that what might be disorganization for you may be working for them. For example, many Intuitives, especially *NP*s, organize papers in piles rather than files. If they can find the papers they need and complete tasks by deadline, support their way of organization.

- Don't assume that you are responsible for *N*s' organization or lack thereof. You do not have to keep track of details, papers, etc., for them unless they ask and you agree.

- Ask clarifying questions when you are assigned a task in a vague way: how long, how detailed, how many copies, and the like. However, don't panic if all the details aren't forthcoming immediately—they simply may not be known yet. You may need to plunge ahead on your own, seeking more clarification later.

Thinking (T) — Feeling (F)

Thinking types and Feeling types will manage time with a very different focus. *T*s focus on task and efficiency and feel uncomfortable when people try to pull them off task. They want to complete the task first and then deal with people issues. For Feeling types, task completion is important, but paying attention to the people and **how** people interact doing the work is foremost.

THINKING

Strengths:

- set clear priorities
- analyze and assess tasks
- develop structures to keep things moving and complete projects efficiently
- are able to detach from what other people want in order to focus on tasks

Potential problems:

- may have trouble accepting that some things seem illogical but still need to be done
- may put off things that involve interpersonal interactions
- focus on efficiency, which can lead to ignoring people's needs
- may forget to include time for personal interactions, coaching, and relationship building

Tips

For Thinking types . . .

- Remember, if you don't deal with interpersonal relationships in a timely way, they can interfere with efficient task completion. A management group of Thinking types who are making restructuring decisions without including information about what the impact will be on the people affected may find that their decision-making and planning time was all wasted. As one group said, "It all blew up in our faces, and we had to go back to square one."
- Thinking is often the accepted mode of time management in an organization. Recognize that this is not the natural way for all people. Just because it's supported by the organization doesn't mean one should automatically operate that way all the time.
- Thinking types can offer their ability to structure and prioritize tasks to assist others in their work.

For those who work with Thinking types . . .

- Recognize that their task focus is natural and efficient for them. It's not necessarily that they are trying to avoid people issues. Ask for the time you need to process interpersonal issues; make clear the urgency of the issue, e.g., "I can't contribute further until we talk about these things." That gets the Thinker's attention.
- Ask Thinkers how they see the priorities and how to structure the next steps. They will usually be glad to give you this information.

FEELING

Strengths:

- respond to others' needs for time—make a priority of the needs of people who are important to them
- prioritize tasks by their own value system and commitments to people or ideals
- facilitate others in achieving their goals
- go beyond the call of duty to support their cause

Potential problems:

- may put other people's priorities before their own
- may let worries about harmony take precedence over getting the task done
- may let their need to talk about what is happening to them and others get in the way of task completion
- may put people's immediate needs ahead of future perspective

Tips

For Feeling types . . .

- Pay attention to your own insights about what is going on for people and yourself. Learn to distinguish between those that are necessary to discuss in order for the work to continue and those that may be better dealt with later.
- Take the risk of communicating your important observations about impacts on people, even though this may disrupt the task-completion process and make others uncomfortable.

- Learn to say no. An intermediate step may be to say, "Let me think about that." Then think what the effect will be on your schedule.

For those who work with Feeling types . . .

- Recognize their need for interpersonal connection before task. This can be as brief as, "Hi, did you have a good weekend?"
- Recognize that their insights about people can be very helpful to you in acknowledging the impact of your work on others, thereby saving you grief in the long run.
- When a feeling type says, "We need to look at this now," make that part of your task.

Judging (J)—Perceiving (P)

This is the preference that most directly and obviously relates to time management. Both J and P are ways of organizing work and getting tasks done, but most time-management systems focus on the J way and view the P way as a *lack* of time management.

JUDGING

Strengths:

- focus on completion, willing to close off and move on
- organized
- plan both in short and long range
- file things
- structure time
- follow through consistently

- see the subtasks to getting things done
- make and follow agendas
- develop routines that save time

Potential problems:

- may not gather enough information before finishing a task and end up having to redo the task to make it right
- may finish something that has become irrelevant
- can't let go until it's done—even when the deadline is far away or the task is unimportant
- expect others to do things their way—force their own ways on others, not allowing for others to use their own styles

Tips

For Judging types . . .

- Keep up the good work but don't insist that everybody works the way you do. Recognize that your needs for structure are not shared by everyone, so don't impose your structure on others unless they ask for it.

- Be careful not to organize and complete a task too quickly, before you've considered what other information needs to be gathered or possibilities for doing it a better way. Don't seal and mail that envelope—you may think of something else that needs to go in!

- Build in time for fun, for playfulness. Judging types often say that they can't play until the work is done; yet, without breaks, they may lose effectiveness and perspective.

- Be willing to reconsider decisions once they've been made. It may seem to be a waste of time to you, but be respectful when other people need to reopen a discussion or revisit a conversation. It may save time in the long run by resulting in a more balanced, informed decision.

For those who work with Judging types . . .

- Communicate your own way of structuring and completing tasks.
- Don't be flattened by the steamroller effect of Judging in action. Feel comfortable saying, "I'm not yet ready to make a decision or close that off." Ask for more time, and if you can, even specify how much more time you need.
- Ask for support for doing it your way. You need not be apologetic about your methods as long as you turn in good work on time.
- Ask *J*s to help you structure a project and establish a timeline.

PERCEIVING

Strengths:

- have an inner timing mechanism that indicates when it is time to move into high gear
- can do multiple tasks at once
- can juggle time—push deadlines, discard unnecessary pieces
- handle surprises and last-minute changes
- work with amazing efficiency under a time crunch—get energy from a deadline

Potential problems:

- may not have developed and learned to trust their timing mechanism
- may get defensive about their way of structuring work
- may unduly delay the task until the information is complete—"I have just one more question. . . ."
- may unduly stress others who prefer structure and time frames
- may seem to others to be avoiding their responsibilities

Tips

For Perceiving types . . .

- Speak up when you see that more reflection and data gathering are needed. This can save time in the long run.
- Don't compare your organizing style to that of *J*s, to your detriment.
- Learn to trust and listen to your timing mechanism.
- Don't let your rebellion to the time frames and structuring of the J way get in the way of your own completion of the task.

For those who work with Perceiving types . . .

- Close your eyes to the process. Evaluate by the final result.
- Set a real deadline (not an artificial one) and communicate its importance clearly. Expect the P to live up to it.
- Appreciate their flexibility and their ability to respond to

emergencies—they can always "make the time" to handle an emergency.

- Enjoy their way of making work more fun. Remember that they tend to merge work and play and find ways to make work playful.

- Confront *P*s if their behavior has negatively impacted your ability to complete your task.

Adding Psychological Type to Time Management in Action

Judith (INTJ) is given the assignment to develop a written report recommending a significant restructuring of a large department. Laura (INTP) will work with her. The staff has been discussing this off and on for some weeks, and they feel that the time has arrived to put the ideas on paper, devise a plan for implementing, and move ahead. Judith and Laura agree that they can complete their written recommendations in two weeks.

They have their preliminary meeting on Monday and Judith says, "I have a pretty good idea of what we need to do; how about if we get the general picture down on paper and then divide up the pieces to flesh them out." She begins writing due dates in her Day-Timer and starts a "to do" list.

Laura asks Judith to elaborate on her ideas, or Judith says, "Let me spell out some of my ideas." (As two people preferring Introversion and Thinking, Judith and Laura both tend to do things their own way, develop their own ideas. At this point, working together would be facilitated by modifying their styles to seek and communicate additional information from each other.)

Laura says, "You know, since we started talking about this in the department, I've noticed some very interesting books on 'reengineering' corporations. I think they've got some interest-

ing ways of approaching these questions that can help us think about possibilities and also give us some logic and support for what we recommend."

Laura adds, "I want to spend time researching these ideas during the week and then put some ideas down on paper over the weekend in time for our meeting next Monday." *(Laura gives Judith information about her own natural style of gathering information and playing around with ideas first, then putting her thoughts down on paper—this is Laura's NP style, and is quite different from Judith's natural NJ style. Judith needs and deserves this information.)*

Judith: "Well, I think we basically know what we need to recommend, but if you want to spend some time putting a few ideas together first, that would be fine with me. Can you write up some of the ideas and put them in a rough outline?"

Laura: "Sure, I can do that. Actually, it will be kind of fun. I've been wanting to get into this stuff."

Judith adds, "You know, once I get a clear picture of how something needs to be, I'm generally ready to move ahead and finish it off. I hear you wanting to add additional information—my natural tendency is to say, 'That's a waste of time,' but I'll do my best to stay open to any new perspectives you think will be helpful." *(Judith explains her own NJ style to Laura, information that will help her understand Judith's reactions. Judith also shows a willingness to modify her own natural style in order to take advantage of what Laura has to offer—she remembers Laura's good work on other projects.)*

Tuesday and Wednesday, Judith notices that Laura has more and more books piled on her desk, with more and more bookmarks and Post-it notes in them. At various times, she notices Laura animatedly explaining things to various people. From what she overhears, Laura is telling people about someone's theories, reading quotes from various books, and the like. She does not see Laura writing at her computer.

Judith's natural tendency is to react like this: By Thursday, Judith is getting nervous. She says to Laura, "How are you coming on that outline? Let me see your preliminary work, so we can see if we're thinking along the same lines." Laura, of course, would have to admit that she has nothing on paper. **However, since Laura explained her style and approach to Judith, Judith can recognize that Laura is in her information-gathering mode. She may ask, "How's it going?" and Laura might explain some of the ideas she's gathering. Judith may notice her own nervousness with Laura's style and want something else, but she can see it for what it is—if she were in Laura's shoes and acting this way, she would be nervous at the delay!**

Or Judith may simply remain detached from what Laura's doing and go about her own responsibilities. Either way, there's no implication of "checking up on Laura" or "being let down," and since Judith has not been "checking up," Laura is not feeling pushed or resentful.

Laura says, "I heard yesterday about an excellent book that's just out, and really pulls all this stuff together. I called and it's not in the library or bookstore yet, but then I called the publisher and they're sending it to me Express Mail. I should get it by tomorrow and then this weekend I'll pull it all together." **Judith says, "Great; is there anything I can do?" Laura feels comfortable saying, "No, I think this is all going to come together nicely."**

In this revised version with Judith and Laura using type knowledge to manage their timing and structuring differences, none of the following happens: Judith feels totally let down. It appears to her that this will be another time when someone fails to follow through, when, if the job is to be done right and on time, she will have to do it herself. She walks away without a word, goes into her office, and writes out the outline she already had in her mind on Monday. Friday morning, she *gives it to Laura and says, "Here, why don't you work from this. Put in the stuff you've been reading and run off a couple of copies and we'll be ready for our Monday meeting."*

Instead, the scenario has the following ending: Judith feels a little uncomfortable with what seems to her the overly open, casual approach Laura is taking, but she reminds herself that Laura works differently and is also effective. Judith and Laura joke about the "pile city" that has developed on Laura's desk and how Express Mail has changed our lives, and Judith says, "I hope the staff appreciates this hot-off-the-press info."

None of this happens either: Laura is incensed. She thinks: If Judith was going to do it herself, why did she agree to work with me? She had already decided what the plan should be and didn't want any additional information. People are coming up with a lot of new, interesting ideas about structuring organizations, and she doesn't care about any of them. I might as well not be a part of this, and I really don't want to because I'm sure her plan won't work—it doesn't take into account any of what's going on now or what's needed in the future. She can do it herself.

Instead, over the weekend, Laura does her reading, then sits down at her computer Sunday afternoon. She draws on (1) the burst of energy that she always gets as deadlines approach and (2) the organizing and structuring that have been going on internally during her reading. On Monday morning, Judith is relieved and pleased to get an in-depth, concise, and interesting analysis of the current "best thinking" about restructuring organizations and work. Judith is able to see quickly how this relates to and provides some additional fleshing out and support for the ideas she has, and the two settle down to figure out how to prepare and present an excellent report.

In the case of Judith and Laura, the primary changes we have made in the situation are fairly simple:

1. Each understands her own natural and best way of organizing a project and structuring her time.
2. Each is prepared to communicate her own most effective style to the other.
3. Each is prepared to modify her own style slightly to meet the legitimate needs of the other.

Improving Your Time-Management Skills

The general principles for using psychological type to assist you in any work activity are the same:

- Figure out your own best way of doing things, learn to build on your strengths, and find props to help you in your weak areas.
- Look at your impact on others and communicate, adjust, or negotiate to insure that you **and others** are getting what you need to do your best work.

Specifically, try the following to help with time management:

1. Become knowledgeable about your personality and time-management style—learn what works for you and what doesn't.

- What are some things that you do to manage your time that work?
- What are some things that you've tried that don't work for you?
- Does knowing your type help you understand why things have worked or not?
- Think of a time when you were most productive and effi-

cient, and then try to determine what factors in that situation allowed you to manage your time so well. What can you learn from that?

• Recognize also that assets can turn into liabilities. If you are someone for whom interruptions are exciting and stimulating most of the time (such as an ENFP), keep that as part of your style. However, if you are under a time crunch, the interruptions may not be so welcome and you may have to ignore them.

2. Seek information from others about the impact of your time-management style on them.

• Ask others directly. Mention a recent task that you worked on together and ask what about your style worked for them and what they found difficult.

• If you are a person who is energized by an upcoming deadline (like the INTP in our example), but find it difficult to complete work until that deadline is in sight, check out whether that works for those with whom you'll be working. For some people, this may cause excessive stress as they scramble to build on your work.

3. Be clear in communicating your style to others who are affected by it.

• Sometimes our style is so obvious to us that we don't realize that others do not understand it. This is particularly noticeable in the Judging-Perceiving dimension.

• Judging types inherently create a structure and a time frame for their work, and may fail to communicate to Perceiving types the importance of this to their time-management style.

4. Ask for what you need and negotiate for what's possible.

- Two trainers in different cities were to facilitate a session together. Six weeks before the session, the ENFJ called the ENFP and explained that she would like to divide up their responsibilities as soon as possible so she could begin preparing. The ENFP felt uncomfortable being locked into a structure that far ahead of time, but agreed to do so with the caveat that perhaps once they were at the session they could revisit their decisions.

5. Set up some props to help yourself in your weak spots.

- Intuitives may underestimate how long tasks will take. One asks himself, "Now, the last time I did this, how long did it take?" Another asks herself, "Now, how much time will this *really* take?" before agreeing to go ahead on a project with a given timetable.
- One Sensor found it impossible to concentrate as long as he had a messy desk; he solved the problem by finding a clear table in the conference room to work on so he could go ahead with an important project and not get bogged down in cleaning his desk.

6. If your style works for you and doesn't impact others negatively, keep it.

- One ESTP career army sergeant said after learning about psychological type, "I'm no longer going to feel guilty about my 'piled high' desk. I've always been told, 'This isn't the army way.' But it works for me and I get all my stuff done. I'm going to quit trying to change myself."

CHAPTER 4

MEETINGS

Meeting Management in Action

Cast of characters:
George, ESTP, manager
Jane, ESFJ
Randy, ISTJ
Miguel, ENTP
Tom, ENFP
John, ESTJ
Harriet, ESTJ

t was 9 A.M. on Monday. The staff gathered for their weekly meeting. As usual, not everyone was there on time and they were waiting. John said, "What are we doing today?" Harriet answered, "Well, the weekly updates; I don't know what else." Finally George, the manager, said, "I guess we better get started even though Tom and Jane aren't here. We'll start off with updates. Then we've got a couple of production prob-

82

lems we need to discuss. And we'll see if anyone has any other problems we need to deal with. Harriet, start us off."

Harriet gave a brief update about her areas of responsibility.

Jane came in at 9:30, apologizing breathlessly, "I'm sorry, I had to drop my son off at school and then there was an accident on the expressway. . . . What's happened so far?"

George: "Well, Harriet just gave us her update. Things seem to be going okay. She said . . ."

Jane: "Where's Tom?"

George: "I don't know. Has anyone heard from Tom?" Silence.

Randy: "Off on some wild goose chase, probably."

Harriet: "He'll have a good excuse, you can bet on that."

The meeting continued. Randy gave his report and went on and on, as usual. He told them everything he'd done in the last week, everything he planned to do this week. There were side conversations between Miguel and Jane. John was going through his letters and making notes for responses. Harriet was checking her Day-Timer.

Tom came in, saying he was sorry he'd held things up, but he had called back East from home and "got caught in a long conversation—but I think we'll get a big contract out of this."

Harriet said, "Right. Like we got big contracts out of last week's phone call and the one that made you late the week before." Others laughed, and then continued with their reports.

When it got to be John's turn, he said, "Before I give you an update, I've got to tell you that Jack is not working out as the new receptionist. I'm not getting my messages. My best client called the other day, and Jack didn't come and find me. He takes long breaks and sometimes when I come out to tell him something, he hangs up quickly—I'm sure he's been making a personal call."

People were suddenly energized—everyone had something to say.

Randy: "When Ethel was there, that never happened. She always made sure I got my messages and reminded me if I hadn't returned important calls."

Tom: "I heard he has problems at home."

Harriet: "Well, I'm sorry, but he needs to do his job. I mean, we're not a welfare agency here."

Miguel: "Right. He can write to an advice column like Ann Landers about his problems."

Harriet: "George, can you take care of this?"

George: "Well, I guess I could talk with him. Jane, maybe you could have lunch with him, find out what's going on. You're better at that stuff than I am."

John gave his update and everyone settled back into their listening mode. Then it was Miguel's turn, and he told the group he was having real problems with getting the company's annual report printed:

"Two problems have developed. For several weeks, we've been struggling with our paper supplier. They are sending the wrong stuff, or sending the right stuff in the wrong weight, or sending it late. Now they're saying they don't know when they can deliver the paper we've chosen for the report. Then, the finance people keep sending revised figures. We get everything typeset and send it to them for final proofing, and they send back new numbers.

"It's gotten so bad that I'm really worried about delivering the report on time. And we know what will happen if it's not done right and on time."

The group began problem-solving:

"Have you checked to find out what's going on with the paper supplier? Have you told them that they've got to shape up or we'll find another supplier? I mean, we give them a lot

of business; I'd think a little pressure would change the behavior."

"Those finance people will drive you crazy. All they care about is that their numbers are exact. I bet a lot of the changes aren't even important ones, right?"

"That's right. For instance, their original numbers maybe said $92,000, and then their final refiguring comes out with $91,700, and they want to change it to $91,700. I mean, nobody reads those numbers anyway."

Suddenly, Tom looked at his watch and said, "I've got a ten-thirty appointment with the PR folks that I can't miss. I'm going to have to run."

Everyone started gathering their things together and saying, "Yeah, me too, I've got to . . ." As she left, Jane said, "Miguel, let me know if I can help."

George and Miguel were left in the room, with George saying, "Miguel, you're just going to have to take charge here. That report's got to be done right and on time, no matter what."

As they walked down the hall, John and Harriet agreed that it had been another wasted morning. "These staff meetings mean I always start the week behind. I don't know why George can't just take care of this stuff."

If you could rewrite this meeting, what would you do differently?

How do you deal with chronic latecomers such as Tom?

How would you have handled Randy's inappropriately long and detailed report?

How could you have given Miguel's problems the attention they need?

The Importance of Meeting Management

In most organizations, people spend 25 to 75 percent of their time in meetings and working in teams.[1] Recommendations for "reengineering" organizations—from empowering employees to total quality management—emphasize working in teams, group decision-making, and group responsibility. Yet when faced with meetings, most people say to themselves, "Oh no, another meeting. I've got so many meetings I can't get my work done." Meetings seem to be an "add-on" instead of a place where productive work happens.

Why do people dread and dislike meetings? Maybe these comments from others echo some of your feelings about meetings:

- "Nothing gets done—they're a waste of time."
- "They're totally task-focused; there's no time for process, to discuss issues fully, offer ideas"; or "They're all process with no action and no closure on topics."
- "We spent two hours deciding something I could have decided in five minutes."
- "Some people are like a broken record—whatever the topic, once they start, everyone knows what they will say and tunes out."
- "People don't speak up, don't disagree in the meeting, then they say what they really think outside in the halls."
- "Some people talk all the time; others don't speak."
- "There's a small group who makes the decisions anyway—they ask us, but it doesn't matter what we think."
- "The agenda's not relevant to me or my work" or "There is no agenda"—"I don't know why I'm here."

- "The purpose is not clear—did they just want to give information or were we supposed to decide something?"
- "The meeting seems like a token gesture, a meaningless attempt to 'include' people."

We believe another reason why meetings don't work is because they do not recognize and support individual differences. The standard ways of meeting management seem to meet the needs of people with certain preferences and not others, and allow some people to get what they want and make a contribution while presenting a real challenge for people with other preferences. In our view, the typical ways of handling meetings encourage the following:

Extraversion: **They recommend that everyone participate in a way that includes**

- spontaneity
- contributing freely, bringing up objections—immediately
- being energetic and forceful in presentations
- holding nothing back

Thinking: **They recommend that the business of the meeting be approached in a way that includes**

- a task-focused, technical (focus on the work) approach
- a problem-solving approach
- use of detached critiquing and analysis
- questioning
- using logic and systems

Judging: **They recommend a structure that involves**

- tight time frames
- keeping to schedule
- working through until finished
- making decisions
- being organized—staying on topic
- *closure:* action plans, steps; who will do what, when

What's wrong with this? Nothing in itself, but methods that don't take individual differences into account don't work for everyone. Every perspective is important. Even groups that don't include people with all preferences will find that their meetings result in more effective decisions because of the balanced perspective provided by taking all the preferences into account.

Type and Meeting Management

Psychological type provides a way to understand the needs and contributions of different people to the work of groups. Making use of this perspective and knowledge will allow us to design meetings and participate in groups in ways that will work better for everyone and allow everyone to contribute. Everyone present, not just the leader, has a responsibility for insuring that a meeting is productive.

Extraversion (E) — Introversion (I)

When **Extraverts** go to meetings, they want

- a chance to see people and interact with them

- to talk over ideas and work together on projects—they find this energizes and stimulates them
- a break in their day
- a chance to be involved in the action—whatever it is

When **Introverts** go to meetings, they want

- advance notice of topics so they can prepare ahead of time, think over the issues
- a group where they feel comfortable talking (usually a smaller group of people they know)
- time for internal processing, then airtime for their reflections
- in-depth focus on a subject
- a chance to share their knowledge and information
- to stabilize and calm a group—ask, "What are we overlooking?"

As you read through this list, you'll notice that meetings provide Extraverts with a lot of what they want while they challenge Introverts to get what they need in order to contribute to the group process. Extraverts have a natural advantage in group settings. The challenge for those setting up meetings and those participating in them is to provide what Introverts need to be effective group members.

PRODUCTIVE MEETINGS FOR BOTH EXTRAVERTS AND INTROVERTS

*E*s and *I*s do not necessarily need *equal* airtime, but to get the best from both, you do need to incorporate a few techniques:

1. Provide an agenda or a list of topics ahead of time.
2. Give advance notice to anyone who will present a specific topic ("Bob, could you give a five-minute summary of how you solved the supply problem in your group?").
3. Use a carousel technique: Before leaving a topic, ask if anyone has any further questions, contributions, or problems, and go quickly around the group, getting a response from everyone ("No, that's it for me," "Well, there was one issue I wanted to mention," etc.).
4. Remember, Extraverts need time to talk an idea through. A group can label this "thinking-out-loud time" and include it in the structure.
5. Watch out for the tendency of some enthusiastic Extraverts to take too much airtime. The group needs to agree on a signal (like a rap on the table) for letting individuals know that they are taking too much group time.
6. Watch out for the tendency of some Introverts to tune out, especially when they are not given an opportunity to communicate their ideas or knowledge.

Sensing (S) — Intuition (N)

What kinds of information do Sensors and Intuitives want to give and hear in a meeting? How do they want information presented?

Sensors prefer

- real, practical information presented in a straightforward way
- sequential presentation—beginning, middle, then end
- keep it short, make it relevant, stay on topic
- clear decisions—What is the decision exactly?
- steps—Who's going to do it? When?
- Remember SWAT (Sensors Want Action Today): If we

talked about it and nothing happens, the meeting was a waste of time (it's okay if we talked and decided not to do anything—that's an action)

- the historical perspective, the lessons of past experience, what others have done
- realism about resources and time frames
- continuity—keeping what's good about past and present as we make changes

Intuitives prefer

- the big picture—the overall framework
- information about how everything connects to everything else
- to know what's the meaning of the topic; does the meaning hang together for me?
- discussion of motivations and theories; what's behind an issue?
- opportunities for creative exploration of new possibilities
- long-term pictures
- brainstorming and "out-of-the-box" thinking ("out-of-the-box" means stepping outside of the way people currently define or understand the issues and trying to see them from another perspective)

PRODUCTIVE MEETINGS FOR Ss AND Ns

Make sure Sensors and Intuitives can contribute in meetings by following these guidelines:

1. Give Intuitives the framework, the overall view at the beginning, like the chapter headings and subheadings in

a book or the topic sentence in a paragraph. For example: "This meeting is to review our personnel forms in light of our new hiring policies." Then you might say, "We're going to look at the application forms, the performance evaluation forms, the probation forms, and the dismissal forms and decide what to do with each of them," which adds more specific Sensing information to the framework.

2. Keep the framing short and keep focused on the business of the meeting. In the above example, know that Intuitives may want to get into the theories behind the new hiring policies, the greater meanings illustrated by them, and how the new policies fit the global shift in employment trends. The Sensor wants to focus on the forms, who will make the changes, when they need to be done, and disseminating them to those who'll use them. Intuitives do need some "theorizing time," with an agreement to do so for a specified time period (like ten minutes), and then move to the tasks at hand.

3. Use type to help you identify the relevant task at hand—do you need to focus more on the Intuitive big picture or the Sensing details? One may be more pertinent than the other; the important thing is to be clear.

4. Sensors typically respond to a new idea by going back through their experience to find relevant information about it. Some become historians for the group, reminding them of when this was tried before, what the results were, problems that arose, etc. Intuitives may be bored with this, finding that getting into this "ancient" history is irrelevant and a waste of time. Intuitives typically use a new idea as a springboard to generate possibilities. They see their ideas as connected to the topic and deserving of exploration. Sensors may believe this is rushing

ahead before there's a real understanding of the issues at hand. This natural difference can be very frustrating to both but important information can be missed without allowing for both. Some groups have dealt with this by labeling time periods ("Now it's Intuitive time"; "Now it's Sensing time"), thus supporting the value of both ways of approaching information and decisions and also insuring that both types remain invested in the discussion. Make it clear that "Intuitive time" includes Sensors using their Intuition, and vice versa.

5. Build in a time at the end of meetings to clarify and identify the specific decisions made and steps that will be taken. The new ideas discussed and possible avenues for future exploration can also be identified.

Thinking (T)—Feeling (F)

Meetings frequently are for the purpose of making decisions. The T-F preference focuses on what information needs to be included in group decisions, what process will be followed in decision-making, and what principles and values will direct the decision-making.

Thinkers prefer to step back and use an objective viewpoint in decision-making. In meetings, Thinkers prefer to

- focus on tasks in a technical, detached way
- analyze and critique
- include only the "right" data—data that's "relevant," precise
- be brief and efficient
- get to the core and stay focused
- assess cause and effect

- show their competence and knowledge
- use a little "T humor" (which can take several forms: sarcastic, biting put-downs, or clever wordplays, or quick retorts and comments on what's illogical)
- use a logical decision-making structure

Feelers prefer to focus on the impacts of decisions on people and to weigh everything by their values. In meetings, Feelers prefer to

- notice explicitly who is there and who is not, and what's happening to people
- discuss the impacts of decisions on people who are involved or affected
- recognize and appreciate people's individual contributions to the meeting
- seek out minority views—be sure everyone is included
- assess if *what* the group is deciding and *how* they are going about the decision are congruent with their values
- find a consensus that honors everyone's perspective

PRODUCTIVE MEETINGS FOR BOTH *T*S AND *F*S

Most organizations value and support the T perspective and overlook or downplay the F perspective. Once people learn about psychological type, the advantages of balancing the two approaches to decision-making become apparent.

1. The best decisions will include both perspectives. As with S and N, some groups have found it useful to designate a specific time for Thinking concerns and another for Feeling perspectives. Both approaches need to be

given weight and used to balance the other. For *T*s, the point may need to be made that it is logical to consider impacts on people and that hearing everyone's viewpoint will result in a better decision.

2. Feeling types need to be willing to take the risk and create disharmony by raising the issue of the impact of decisions on people and on themselves. If they don't, some Feeling types may withdraw, shut down, and the group will lose their input.

   Because T is the accepted way of making decisions in most organizations, *F*s may have learned that their perspectives are not welcome. Coupled with an F's preference to keep things harmonious, this can lead to the *F*s keeping quiet and not taking the risk of speaking out. *F*s need to look at the cost to people they care about and support if they **don't** surface the issue and how strongly they hold the value of caring and supporting those people.

   Thinking types need to acknowledge this F contribution as being important for the group.

3. Often in meetings, "T humor" emerges. This type of humor may take several forms. If the form is somewhat biting, perhaps sarcastic, and focused on one-upmanship, the *F*s listening to it often take offense or are uncomfortable, even when the humor is not directed at them. For *T*s, this type of humor seems to be a form of connecting to others, and they enjoy it immensely. However, because the impact is so negative on *F*s, it might be best if that T humor were curtailed or at least directed at oneself, not others. Some groups handle this by clearly labeling the humor as "T humor" so that everyone understands quickly what is happening and that no offense is meant.

4. Groups, especially those who work together regularly, need to include time for periodically assessing the effectiveness of the process being used in their meetings. Questions might include, "Have we provided airtime for everyone? Is everyone getting the information they need? Anything we need to spend more time or less time on? Have the decisions we've made considered your views?"

5. *F*s often provide the natural glue in a group by asking about and acknowledging issues that are important to individuals. Their role as facilitators of relationships needs to be explicitly recognized and appreciated for its contribution to the group's forming, functioning, and effectiveness.

6. In order for decisions to be truly agreed upon (and bought into) by everyone, differences of opinions must be acknowledged. Groups need to discuss and decide how much agreement is necessary before the group moves on. Some groups ask those who are not comfortable with a decision, "What do you need in order to feel differently?"

Judging (J)—Perceiving (P)

This preference refers to how a meeting will be organized. How will we structure our discussions and decision-making? How will we deal with time? How will we handle emerging information and ideas?

Judgers want

- a clear structure for the meeting, i.e., an agenda
- a time frame that will work, is realistic
- to stick to and complete the agenda and time frame

- clear decisions and closure on each topic, as well as to the meeting
- clarity about when decisions are not appropriate and must be delayed
- attention to development of follow-up plans: who, what, when, why, what's next

Perceivers want

- to keep the time frame open—to explore and play around with the pieces
- to gather and present all available information on the topic
- opportunities to reopen and revisit decisions—to keep things open to new information
- to consider all alternatives
- to delay decisions that feel premature to them
- to reevaluate plans and make midcourse adjustments
- to have some fun—include humor and playfulness
- a decision to emerge from the information and discussion: "If we talk about this long enough, we'll know what we need to do."

PRODUCTIVE MEETINGS FOR BOTH *J*s AND *P*s

Organizations favor Judging. Perceiving types have usually learned many Judging skills and may not have learned to maximize their own natural strengths.

1. Both *J*s and *P*s have developed inner senses of timing that they have learned to trust and use. Unfortunately, meetings in today's organizations generally have such tight time frames that neither type is free to exercise its timing mechanisms. Many decisions end up being closed prematurely for all types.

   Reconsider the purpose of your meeting and the time frame you have established, then see if you can rethink your purpose or adjust your time frame to allow a more natural process.

2. *J*s can use their sense of timing to know when they have heard enough information, then offer their sense of where the decision is. They then need to ask, "Does this fit for everyone?" and be prepared to allow more time if the group is not ready to close on the topic.

3. *P*s can use their sense of timing to say, "It seems to me that we don't have enough information to make this decision today. Does everyone feel okay about postponing the decision until our next meeting?" Then they need to listen to the group. If the group agrees, they need to ask, "How will we gather more information before the next meeting?"

4. *P*s need to speak up when a decision is being made that feels premature to them. Their interjection needs to identify as clearly as possible what additional data is needed before a good decision can be made.

5. Especially in the rapidly changing organizational environment, *P*s need to be encouraged to use their natural ability to suggest midcourse corrections and changes, to bring up new information, and to. challenge the status quo when it's not working.

6. J-P interactions sometimes take on a Parent (J)–Child (P) or Teacher (J)–Student (P) quality (with both sides play-

ing their part with enthusiasm). If at all possible, these old patterns and the accompanying emotions need to be kept out of collegial interactions. Both J and P have much to contribute. However, if *J*s push too hard, too fast, the result is premature closure, which serves no purpose beyond having a decision. If *P*s push too hard for more information, their endless data gathering may make the group miss the window of opportunity for a decision.

7. A possible compromise, when *J*s and *P*s simply cannot agree on whether it is time to make an important decision: Use a pilot program. This gives *J*s a decision and action, while giving *P*s the sense that everything isn't decided, that adjustments can be made.

Adding Psychological Type to Meeting Management in Action

Revisiting the Example

*It was 9 A.M. on Monday. The staff had gathered for their weekly meeting. As usual, not everyone was there on time and they were waiting. John said, "What are we doing today?" Harriet answered, "Well, the weekly updates; I don't know what else." (**Has anyone asked, "Does weekly updating by everyone need to be done in a group meeting or is this simply based on George's Extraverted and Sensing needs?" A note here: The agenda has not been distributed or posted, failing to give the Introverts any advance notice. It would be particularly helpful to send out a note about any unusual items or problems on the agenda.**)*

Finally George, the manager, said, "I guess we better get started even though Tom and Jane aren't here. We'll start off with updates. Then we've got a couple of production problems we need to discuss. And we'll see if anyone has any other problems we need to deal with. Harriet, start us off." **(Note that George doesn't prioritize the agenda items, nor does anyone in the group mention the priority that may need to be given to the production problems. This is usually a contribution made by a Thinking and Judging perspective—why is this group not making use of it? Also, no one seems concerned why Tom and Jane are missing—any F perspectives here?)**

Harriet gave a brief update about her areas of responsibility.

Jane came in at 9:30, apologizing breathlessly. "I'm sorry; I had to drop my son off at school and then there was an accident on the expressway. . . . What's happened so far?"

George: "Well, Harriet just gave us her update. Things seem to be going okay. She said . . ." **(Note: When a person comes late, it is inappropriate to take group time to "catch them up." That is overuse of the Extraverted approach. Jane will need to meet with George later to hear his expectations about timeliness for the Monday meeting and to receive any information she missed.)**

Jane: "Where's Tom?" **(Finally, the F perspective!)**

George: "I don't know. Has anyone heard from Tom?" Silence.

Randy: "Off on some wild goose chase, probably."

Harriet: "He'll have a good excuse, you can bet on that."

(Note: A little "T humor," which probably leaves at least Jane feeling uncomfortable and wishing she hadn't asked the question.)

The meeting continued. Randy gave his report and went on and on, as usual. He told them everything he'd done in the last week, everything he planned to do this week. **(Note: Neither George nor the group had dealt with appropriate time frames** *and how to let people know when they were taking too much group time—they need some additional J perspective and some negotiated agreements around agenda and time.) There were side conversations between Miguel and Jane. John was going through his letters and making notes for responses. Harriet was checking her Day-Timer. (Note: Several people may have "checked out" or are simply being rude. The time agreements above, plus ground rules agreed upon by the group [one person talking at a time], may help, but also be aware that some Extraverts like doing several things at the same time, for example, listening while looking at their Day-Timers.)*

Tom came in, saying he was sorry he'd held things up, but he had called back East from home and "got caught in a long conversation—but I think we'll get a big contract out of this."

Harriet said, "Right. Like we got big contracts out of last week's phone call and the one that made you late the week before." Others laughed, and then continued with their reports. (Note: "T humor" again, which has obviously not been effective in dealing with what seems to be a chronic problem for Tom. Could the group possibly use F to focus on the way they work together, especially on discussing the impact of Tom's lateness behavior on the group and how the group wants to deal with this?)

When it got to be John's turn, he said, "Before I give you an update, I've got to tell you that Jack is not working out as the new receptionist. I'm not getting my messages. My best client called the other day, and Jack didn't come and find me. He takes long breaks and sometimes when I come out to tell him something, he hangs up quickly—I'm sure he's been making a personal call."

People were suddenly energized—everyone had something

*to say. (**Note: People have probably been bored by the same
old routine and by excessive listening; they are glad for a
chance to get involved in discussion. However, this is not a
primary agenda item for discussion here. This group meeting
is probably not the best forum for problem-solving a personnel issue.**)*

Randy: "When Ethel was there, that never happened. She always made sure I got my messages and reminded me if I hadn't
returned important calls." (**The ISTJ "good old days" syn-
drome: History can be important, but it isn't here.**)

Tom : "I heard he has problems at home." (**An example of
F identifying with Jack, concerned about him as an individual.**)

Harriet: "Well, I'm sorry, but he needs to do his job. I
mean, we're not a welfare agency here." (**The "tough" T approach.**)

Miguel: "Right. He can write to an advice column like Ann
Landers about his problems." (**A little more "T humor."**)

Harriet: "George, can you take care of this?"

George: "Well, I guess I could talk with him. Jane, maybe
you could have lunch with him, find out what's going on. You're
better at that stuff than I am." (**Whose responsibility is this? Is
George uncomfortable with personal/personnel issues, potentially emotional conversations? Is he trying to hand this off to
an F?**)

*John gave his update and everyone settled back into their
listening mode. (**Boredom setting in again.**) Then it was
Miguel's turn, and he told the group he was having real problems with getting the company's annual report printed:*

"Two problems have developed. For several weeks, we've
been struggling with our paper supplier. They are sending the
wrong stuff, or sending the right stuff in the wrong weight, or
sending it late. Now they're saying they don't know when they

can deliver the paper we've chosen for the report. Then, the finance people keep sending revised figures. We get everything typeset and send it to them for final proofing, and they send back new numbers.

"It's gotten so bad that I'm really worried about delivering the report on time. And we know what will happen if it's not done right and on time." **(Note: This is an issue of great importance to the entire group, yet it comes up toward the end of the meeting—it needed to be dealt with as a high priority item!)**

The group began problem-solving:

"Have you checked to find out what's going on with the paper supplier? Have you told them that they've got to shape up or we'll find another supplier? I mean, we give them a lot of business; I'd think a little pressure would change the behavior."

"Those finance people will drive you crazy. All they care about is that their numbers are exact. I bet a lot of the changes aren't even important ones, right?"

"That's right. For instance, their original numbers maybe said $92,000, and then their final refiguring comes out with $91,700, and they want to change it to $91,700. I mean, nobody reads those numbers anyway." **(Note: This is, in some ways, the "worst" of Intuitive brainstorming. There's no structure or time frame, no plan comes out of it, and no solution is reached. The group needs to apply some S and J!)**

Suddenly, Tom looked at his watch and said, "I've got a ten-thirty appointment with the PR folks that I can't miss. I'm going to have to run." **(Note: The time frame has been undefined from the beginning, so staff members don't know how long to allow for the meeting.)**

Everyone started gathering their things together and saying,

"Yeah, me too, I've got to . . ." **(Note: No closure to the meeting, no summary of what's been learned or decided.)** *As she left, Jane said, "Miguel, let me know if I can help."* **(A little F personal concern, though not focused enough or supported enough by the group to be very helpful.)**

George and Miguel were left in the room, with George saying, "Miguel, you're just going to have to take charge here. That report's got to be done right and on time, no matter what." **(Why does the group meet and do this processing together if the result is that "Miguel will just have to deal with it"?)**

As they walked down the hall, John and Harriet agreed that it had been another wasted morning. "These staff meetings mean I always start the week behind. I don't know why George can't just take care of this stuff." **(John and Harriet's perspective is understandable but not very positive for the group—can the purpose of these meetings be clarified and the structure/agenda redefined to make the meetings productive and worthwhile?)**

As you can see, a lot of what's wrong with this meeting can be understood and corrected by using meeting-management techniques we've discussed in this chapter. The group could also profit from understanding and making productive use of their type differences, instead of allowing those differences to get in the way of their functioning.

The J-P differences in the group seem to be ones the group avoids, perhaps because George, the manager, prefers Perceiving, while the group is primarily Judging. As a result of not surfacing these differences, the group seems not to get the best of Judging *or* Perceiving.

The predominance of the Thinking perspective is also one the group could profit from discussing. The value of a Feeling perspective is recognized only in a rather backhanded way, when George tries to avoid a potentially emotional situation. Could this group find ways to recognize and integrate more F perspectives and processing into their functioning?

Important Points to Remember

Keep these important points about using type in meeting management in mind:

1. Step back to analyze what's missing in your group meetings as we did in our scenario. Psychological type can help identify some of the missing perspectives.
2. Take psychological type into consideration before the meeting (sending out notices about topics), during the meeting (setting clear priorities, agreeing on time frames), and after the meeting (including follow-up plans) to insure that the meeting is most productive for everyone.
3. Good meetings need to allow for the perspectives and contributions of all eight preferences. Groups need action *and* reflection, data *and* possibilities, logic *and* the impact on people, closure *and* openness.
4. Even if your group does not include people with all eight of the preferences, you will function better if all eight preferences and their perspectives are included. For example, if your group is all Thinkers, they will still make better decisions if they learn to ask, "What will be the impact of this on people?" and to pay attention to the answer.
5. When you are the one leading the meeting, assess your own skills so that you know your own strengths and

shortcomings and how they relate to those at the meeting. Know where you might get sidetracked and identify ways you can use type to help you have a more productive meeting.

CHAPTER 5

LEADING:
BEING IN CHARGE

Leaders We Have Known

ill was reminiscing:

"*When I first went to work for this company thirty years ago, I had a wonderful boss. Gary was one of the original founders of the company, along with his brother, and he took on responsibility for hiring people, getting us organized, and making us feel like a part of the family. He worked hard to build consensus so everyone was included, and he always asked each of us what we thought before he made even the smallest decisions. He knew everything about each of us—our birthdays, our families, everything.*

"*Now it's true, if you left him out of the loop, he would get upset and feel hurt. He wasn't great at making the tough decisions—we carried some dead weight that we should have gotten rid of. And every once in a while, he would get on his high horse, shake his finger at us, and say, 'That is just wrong!'*

"When Gary retired, we had a great party for him. Everyone felt sad; it was like losing a wise uncle. It took him a week to pack up all the personal mementos in his office.

"The next boss I had—what a difference! Rob was also very competent, but in a really different way. There wasn't a machine or technical system he couldn't figure out, and if you went to him with a technical problem, he was great—he'd get all involved and work until it was solved. He'd ask lots of questions, but then let you do your job however you wanted. The business was really growing, and he seemed to always be on top of everything—he could pull together and make sense of a ton of information. He was smart, and I learned a lot from him.

"I can think of a number of times, though, when we'd be in a staff meeting and he'd come up with something out of the blue—a totally new direction that he hadn't discussed with anyone. Things were changing quickly, and there were times when we really needed him to tell us what to do, but he'd always say, you guys figure it out. Yet if we went in a direction that didn't match his standards, we'd be in trouble! Sometimes we really had to push him to get a decision on important things.

"When he left the company, he did it suddenly. It seemed like he was here one day and gone the next. We missed him and his technical expertise, but most of us felt that we hadn't ever really known him well.

"Then Catherine came in. I felt pretty uncomfortable at first with a woman boss—remember that was the late nineteen seventies. But pretty quickly, we forgot she was a woman. Tough? Boy, was she tough. And a straight shooter. You always knew where she stood and what she wanted. You went to ask her about something, and she gave you the answer before you'd finished describing the problem. We were really organized and efficient. She streamlined every system, and you could either *get on board or get out of the way. She helped us solidify and set up systems to deal with the growth we'd been experiencing.*

"Of course, some did feel bulldozed by Catherine's style. She was so blunt that she made a lot of people mad, even if she was right. Sometimes she made decisions so quickly that she missed some important information.

"She got a big promotion when she moved on—we weren't surprised—we'd known she was a fast-tracker. She ran a tight ship, and, I must admit, we were ready to loosen up a little. On the other hand, some of us were worried that everything might fall apart.

"Our business really changed in the late eighties and we became much more customer and market focused. It seemed that Vic arrived just in time. The first thing he did was to meet with every person in the department. He spent a lot of time with us, asking questions and finding out about all of us. We started going out to lunch, going out after work together—he was so encouraging, really a good guy. Before we knew it, we had begun feeling like a team! He always said to us, "The only reason we're here is to satisfy our customers. If we don't do that, we might us well close up shop and go home." Our customer-satisfaction ratings really went up.

"I must admit, though, he could drive us crazy. It was hard for some of us to move from Catherine's structured work to Vic's freewheeling style. When tough decisions needed to be made, he kept putting them off, hoping something would happen to resolve them. Sometimes he thought he was being really clear, and we didn't have a clue what he was talking about. He could change his mind three times just walking down the hall to the watercooler—we learned that you wanted to be the last one he talked to! And some people thought he played favorites, and I guess there were some of us who he would talk with and listen to easier than others."

Bill has described four different styles of leading (we use the words *leading* and *leader* in their broadest sense, to include activities of leading, managing, supervising, and team leadership). Each was effective in certain areas; each had its drawbacks for followers. We'll look at the four leaders Bill has described in more depth below. Bill obviously had figured out how to work with each one well, but to give you a head start, we'll also suggest tips to help you deal more effectively with each of these types of leaders.

Some Leadership Styles

Although there are many ways of looking at leadership style, we've chosen four here based on combinations of how leaders make decisions (Thinking or Feeling) and how they deal with their outside worlds (Judging or Perceiving). These two activities are highly important and visible in how we lead and are led.

FJ (ISFJ, ESFJ, INFJ, and ENFJ) Leaders

Gary, Bill's first boss, was an ISFJ, and the style Bill described illustrated many of the strengths and weaknesses we would expect to see in bosses with the combination of Feeling and Judging.

MAJOR CONTRIBUTIONS

- personal vision is tied to their values and beliefs
- others included in decision-making: want to know what others want/need before making decisions and to draw out and involve others
- approachable, want to hear what you have to say

- loyal—very supportive of others and organizational values
- strive for consensus, build it well, and organize the work environment to be harmonious
- want all employees to get what they want and need

MAJOR COMPLAINTS FROM FOLLOWERS

- avoid tough decisions, especially those that will affect people negatively
- don't give the bad news—try to put a positive spin on everything
- may avoid confronting difficult people—will cover up problem people, carry them along
- can become moralistic about their personal values: "This is wrong—I wouldn't ever treat people that way, and you shouldn't either!"
- can focus on relationships to the extent that it interferes with task completion—people issues come first
- want to be included and feel hurt if they are excluded

TIPS FOR DEALING WITH FJ LEADERS

1. Build a relationship with them—find out who they are as people and what's important to them.
2. Give them personal information about yourself.
3. Ask for their advice, help, and support regularly.
4. Include and inform them—don't exclude them, even when it would seem appropriate.
5. To persuade them of your position, don't rely on logical arguments. Tell them why it's important to you as an individual and how this affects you personally as well as why it's helpful to the team.

6. If they have a sensitive area, do your best to avoid it.
7. Use gentle, kind humor (not "T" sarcasm).
8. If they are under stress, recognize that they may be un-movable and back off.

TP (ISTP, ESTP, INTP, and ENTP) Leaders

Bill's second boss, Rob, was an ISTP, and the style Bill described illustrated many of the strengths and weaknesses we would expect to see in bosses with a combination of Thinking and Perceiving.

MAJOR CONTRIBUTIONS

- technical expertise—high standards of competence for themselves and others
- give followers lots of room—hands-off leadership style
- see all information as good and potentially useful
- analyze vast amounts of information, create a logical structure for it
- tolerant of diversity of styles, as long as people get results
- flexible—stay open to new information and directions

MAJOR COMPLAINTS FROM FOLLOWERS

- don't give much direction: "Do it any way you want that works"
- change direction quickly, leaving others confused and seeing them as inconsistent
- may not share their reasons for doing things or their decisions because "it's so obvious"
- oblivious to others' differing needs—can come across as insensitive

- intolerant of those who don't meet their standards and tough on what they see as incompetence
- may put off decisions too long, hoping something will happen to resolve the situation

TIPS FOR DEALING WITH TP LEADERS

1. Give them lots of space to do their own thing.
2. Don't push, especially for decisions they're not ready to make—they'll slide away from you or get angry and push back.
3. Give them the problem, rather than the solution. If they want your solution, they'll ask.
4. Respect their independence and competence and trust them to do their job. Don't look over their shoulder.
5. Be direct and clear in your communication.
6. When you need to give them information about interpersonal problems or conflicts, keep it simple and low-key—present it to them as a problem and ask them to think of a solution.
7. Ask them what you want to know—about their expectations of your work, their sense of the group's direction—rather than waiting for them to share that with you.
8. Accept that you may not get a direct response or step-by-step instructions; they will give more general direction and expect you to figure out how to do a job.

TJ (ISTJ, ESTJ, INTJ, and ENTJ) Leaders

Bill's third boss, Catherine, was an ENTJ, and the style Bill described illustrated many of the strengths and weaknesses we would expect to see in bosses with the combination of Thinking and Judging.

MAJOR CONTRIBUTIONS

- cut to the chase—they get to the point and stay focused
- you know where they stand—they take clear positions
- appear calm, confident, and self-assured
- take quick action to implement decisions
- are fair and consistent—they will have systematic principles and will stick to them
- organize and structure the work to achieve goals

MAJOR COMPLAINTS FROM FOLLOWERS

- leave others out of the decision-making process unless their views are directly relevant
- speak bluntly—can feel to others like a personal attack
- leave others in the dust—may move to action before others are ready (especially the ETJs)
- decide too quickly—may not gather enough information, including the impacts on people
- don't bend the rules for anyone
- so focused on task completion that they won't let go—picture a steamroller!

TIPS FOR DEALING WITH TJ LEADERS

1. Approach them directly with what you want and need, and be ready to provide a logical rationale for it.
2. Organize what you want to say into major points (use bullets if written)—don't ramble!
3. If you need to go to them with a problem, be sure you've

thought it through and tell them what you've tried or want to try.

4. Show them that you are competent and effective—demonstrate timely results.
5. Tell them the consequences you see of their decisions, both positive and negative: "If we do this, this may happen."
6. Stand up to them; they like their ideas but want to be critiqued and don't respect "yes" people.
7. Don't expect a lot of praise or appreciation; recognize that their critiques show they are interested and involved.
8. Recognize that they show their concern for others by problem-solving and that they like to receive acknowledgment from others for how well they solved problems.

Hundreds of studies of the MBTI types of leaders and managers indicate that 60 to 85 percent prefer the combination of Thinking and Judging.[1] This means that there is a good chance you have or will have a TJ boss through much of your work life. Learning to deal more effectively with TJ leaders will make your work life more successful—and more enjoyable!

FP (ISFP, INFP, ESFP, and ENFP) Leaders

Bill's last boss, Vic, was an ESFP, and the style Bill described illustrated many of the strengths and weaknesses we would expect to see in bosses with the combination of Feeling and Perceiving.

MAJOR CONTRIBUTIONS

- seek lots of information about everyone's positions, everything going on
- encourage rather than direct
- support individual differences and styles
- stay flexible, respond to whatever comes up
- involve and energize others
- are resourceful—know whom to contact for help and freely ask for information

MAJOR COMPLAINTS FROM FOLLOWERS

- change directions quickly as new information comes in— may appear inconsistent
- others may not really realize what's important to them because they may not make their central values clear to others
- put off decisions—hope "it will work out"
- avoid tough decisions because they hate disappointing or hurting people
- appear to play favorites—give special treatment to those they like and who like them
- go off in a number of directions that seem like tangents— resist structure

TIPS FOR DEALING WITH FP LEADERS

1. Trust their insights and instincts about people and express this trust to them.
2. Respect their values and what's important to them (you may have to ask to know what this is).
3. Build and maintain a personal connection with them.

4. When you need to present negative feedback, remember that direct criticism doesn't work well. Instead, tell them the personal impact the behavior has on you or others.
5. Trust that their indirect path will eventually lead to the goal.
6. Use light, gentle humor (watch the misuse of "T humor").
7. When they've done something you like, tell them about it.
8. You can't give them too much sincere appreciation.

No matter what types of bosses you have, keep in mind that they have a particular style of leadership and your work life will go much better and be more pleasant if you understand this style and learn to deal with it effectively.

Effective Decision-Making

In addition to assisting you in learning to follow others more effectively, using the theory of type can help when you find yourself in a leadership position, formal or informal. Current changes in organizations and in the nature of work make it likely that each of us will be in situations where we need to use and develop our skills as leaders.

One of the things we most rely upon leaders to do is to make good decisions. Their decisions affect personal as well as organizational well-being, both immediately and in the long term. For many leaders, decision-making is almost automatic—they continue to use their familiar, comfortable approaches. We believe that being knowledgeable about psychological type can help leaders learn to make better decisions.

Experienced and effective leaders have usually learned

some of the approaches we will recommend, though they may not use the same terminology. Others can find new perspectives to improve their decision-making. From a psychological-type perspective, good decision-making requires the use of all eight preferences. The two middle letters of any type are of particular importance when we begin to analyze decision-making styles because they refer to two basic stages involved in every decision: gathering information and arriving at a conclusion.

Isabel Myers developed a way of incorporating these type perspectives into decision-making, a tool commonly known as the "zigzag" model. Following such a model can insure that you cover all the bases (S, N, T, and F) in gathering information and evaluating alternatives:

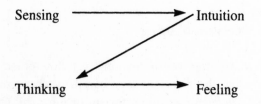

Though you need not follow the model in a linear way, the best decisions will include spending time in each of the perspectives shown in the model: Sensing, Intuition, Thinking, and Feeling.

Questions to Aid Decision-Making

The following gives some suggested ways to include each perspective.

Questions you may want to consider while in the "S" mode:

1. What are the actual concrete facts of the situation?
2. What would common sense suggest about this?
3. What are the costs? What are the benefits?
4. What are we doing now that's working?
5. What has already been tried? How did it work? Can we modify that?
6. What have others done in similar circumstances?

Questions you may want to consider while in the "N" mode:

1. Try reading between the lines—ask, What's really going on beneath the surface?
2. What other ways could we see this?
3. What are some of the new ideas in the field?
4. What patterns are in the data?
5. Are there theoretical models that would help?
6. What unique and different perspective could we use to view this situation?

Questions you may want to consider while in the "T" mode:

1. What's wrong with everything we've considered?
2. What would be the right way to do this?
3. Why would this be the right way?
4. What are the consequences of each alternative?
5. If we step back, what's most logical?
6. Is this a reasonable thing to do?

Questions you may want to consider while in the "F" mode:

1. Have we heard from everyone?
2. What's good about each idea?

3. What's most important to each person?
4. Can we find a way to include what's important for everyone in the decision?
5. What will fit best with the values of the organization?
6. What will best serve the people to be affected?

Decision-Making Styles

As you can readily see, the optimum way to make decisions is to include all of these perspectives. However, if we look at the two middle letters of each type, we can see that each type has a tendency to focus on just two of the perspectives and to slight the other two. Research indicates that this can lead to flawed decision-making.[2]

To understand better what different types emphasize and overlook in decision-making, we will look at each of the four combinations of middle letters (ST, SF, NF, and NT). We will also give an example of how each combination might deal with this particular decision-making situation:

A department manager has been told by upper management that his or her department must cut its expenditures by 20 percent. How would each combination approach deciding how to respond?

SENSING AND THINKING (ST) LEADERS

They pay most attention to	To make decisions, they will typically
• specific, realistic, "hard" data • past experience	• apply current standard operating procedures • use tried and accepted methods

This results in decisions that may be slanted *toward*	Their decision-making style can be problematic
• established practices • the status quo	• when the situation is ambiguous • when qualitative data is important • when novel and innovative approaches are needed • when major transformation is needed

As a result of this natural style, ST managers might approach budget cutting by

1. looking at last year's budget figures to identify any "extras" that could be cut or
2. making across-the-board 20 percent cuts in every category.

SENSING AND FEELING (SF) LEADERS

They pay most attention to	To make decisions, they will typically
• specific information about people in their environment • the opinions and ideas of people who are important to them	• try to find an alternative agreeable to everyone • emphasize the needs of the specific people they have identified as important

This results in decisions that may be slanted *toward*	Their decision-making style can be problematic
• socially desirable solutions	• when they fail to include quantitative data

- decisions that everyone feels at least reasonably good about

- when they emphasize immediate harmony rather than long-term survival
- when novel and innovative approaches are needed
- when major transformations are required

As a result of this natural style, SF managers might approach budget cutting by

1. asking trusted people what they think would be the best way to proceed or
2. having everyone come together and discuss the problem to reach agreement on what the cuts should be.

INTUITION AND FEELING (NF) LEADERS

They pay most attention to

- relevant stories and anecdotes
- imagery, symbols, and metaphors

To make decisions, they will typically

- generate interesting new ways to see the problem—use their insights
- use analogies: "This is like . . ."

This results in decisions that may be slanted toward

- new, novel solutions
- inspirational programs that will create enthusiasm

Their decision-making style can be problematic

- when quantitative data is important
- when adjustment, rather than transformation, is needed
- when standard operating procedures would solve the problem

- when analogies don't explain the situation—it's not comparable to their experience

As a result of this natural style, NF managers might approach budget cutting by

1. using an analogy to get people to think creatively, saying something like, "Think of what people had to do during World War II to survive—they had to melt down pots and pans to provide metal for airplanes. Maybe there's a way we can completely rethink what we do, combine our current resources, and come up with a new design that requires twenty percent less!" or
2. coming up with an ingenious idea, like selling off old equipment, that would allow them to avoid the cuts.

INTUITION AND THINKING (NT) LEADERS

They pay most attention to	**To make decisions, they will typically**
• patterns and meaning they see in the data • the long-range view	• generate and test hypothetical alternatives • judge solutions by their own conceptual framework

This results in decisions that may be slanted toward	**Their decision-making style can be problematic**
• their own system of understanding • overly rational, unifying models	• when the data don't fit their model (pattern) • when adjustment, rather than transformation, is needed

- when their model is flawed
- when they have based their belief patterns on incorrect assumptions

As a result of this natural style, NT managers might approach budget cutting by

1. developing a critique of the directive and writing a concise statement of it for upper management, saying something like, "If we cut every department by twenty percent, we're signing our own death warrant. We need to step back and take a broader view—combine functions, fundamentally reorganize what we do," or
2. suggesting new models for the organization: "What we need is to become a learning organization."

Anyone in a leadership position can benefit from understanding his or her own particular decision-making style, along with its potential blind spots and biases, and appropriate and inappropriate uses.

The other MBTI preferences also can give helpful pointers to those wishing to increase their skills in decision-making and leading. Here are some examples:

- Extraverted leaders may fail to reflect enough on the data and then act impulsively.

- Introverted leaders may fail to gather information from enough people and to communicate as much as their followers would like.

- Judging leaders may prematurely structure situations and push toward closure without considering enough information.

- Perceiving leaders may leave situations open too long, waiting for the answer to emerge, and fail to provide sufficient structure.

The goal in using the concept of type to understand your own leadership style is finding ways to use the natural strengths of all the preferences and insure that you've covered all the bases.

Enhancing Ways of Leading and Following

Leaders and followers have different styles and needs based in part on their personality preferences. Whether you are leading or following, keep these points in mind:

When you are leading, remember:

1. You likely have a preferred style.
2. Being aware of the strengths and limitations of that style may help you avoid mistakes.
3. You may need to take into account the needs of your followers so that they can work better with you.
4. You may need to actively include the use of all the preferences in your decision-making, whether that means making a conscious effort to ask the questions that preference would ask or seeking out people of those preferences.

When you are following, remember:

1. You also likely have a preferred style.
2. Being aware of your type may help you identify more of what you need from your leader.
3. Understanding your leader's style may help you approach your leader in a way that is easier for him/her to understand you.
4. Differences between your type and your leader's type are to be expected and, hopefully, can be managed to the advantage of both parties.

CHAPTER 6

TEAMWORK

A New Team Is Forming

he training and education department was instructed by management to design and offer organization-wide training in new processes that will completely change the way people work. The department manager formed a new self-managed team with responsibility for designing, planning, and implementing the new training. The team members were

David, ISTJ
Joan, ENTP
Ted, ENTJ
Gail, INTJ
Vivian, INFP

They scheduled their first meeting for two days during the next week. In the meantime, the team members began to think about *what needed to happen in that meeting for them to get a good start. Following are descriptions of each member's thoughts.*

David (ISTJ):

I'll bring a list of questions that I need to have answered and as much information on them as I can:

What are the expectations of management?

What has the organization done in the past?

What resources are going to be available to us: people, time, money, equipment?

What experience and expertise does each person on the team have that applies to this task?

What have other organizations like us done in a similar situation?

If I can get concrete, clear answers to each of these questions, I'll be ready to structure our tasks into a step-by-step plan and begin.

Joan (ENTP):

Boy, this is going to be exciting. I'm tired of doing the same training again and again—this is great.

I wonder what these people will be like to work with. I hope they're sharp and creative people—and fun.

I've got some great ideas—I want to get them out on the table.

I'll make some calls to people I know (have heard of) who will have some good ideas about this.

I'll go to the bookstore this weekend and get some books

that will help us get started. If I can bring in some of these ideas, I'll be ready to begin.

Ted (ENTJ):

What are the politics here? Whose support do we already have? Whose do we need to get? We'd better get clear about that first.

We've got three months to come up with a comprehensive training plan for everyone in the organization. I'll list our goals and take my list to the meeting so we're clear about what we need to get done.

We're going to have to move fast.

We're going to have to get right to task. I'll draw up a chart of the goals and the tasks, and then the group can divide them up.

Once we get the goals and structure in place, I'll be set to start.

Gail (INTJ):

We need to get a clear idea about what the organization is going to look like when we're through. I'd like to start by clarifying our vision for the organization.

I'm pretty clear about my vision. I hope I can get it across to the others without too much hassle.

I'll take the company's strategic plan to the meeting so we can figure out how what we're doing fits into that.

Until we get that vision in place, we won't go anywhere, so we need to begin there.

Vivian (INFP):

> *This is a really important program. It's going to make a difference to the organization. We've neglected developing people for too long. It's an exciting opportunity that can have far-reaching impacts.*
>
> *This is so important—I hope everyone else on the team will take it seriously.*
>
> *I wonder what these other people will be like to work with. We'll need to get a clear idea of the roles we're going to play.*
>
> *What can I do to help this group work together better? Maybe we could start with the MBTI to help us understand and communicate better.*
>
> *I know I'll have to push to have us pay attention to how we're going to work together—but it's important to me.*
>
> *Once we discuss these issues, I'll be ready to begin.*

With these very different perspectives and concerns, it's easy to see why teamwork can be so difficult. If any of these people pushes his or her own perspective while denying the validity of the others, this team could turn into a disaster.

It's also easy to see, however, that each individual's perspective offers an important piece of what a team needs in order to function effectively:

David (ISTJ): the realities and structure

Joan (ENTP): excitement and possibilities

Ted (ENTJ): clear goals, structure, and action

Gail (INTJ): long-term vision and strategy

Vivian (INFP): concern for people—on the team and in the organization

This is not everything a team needs to function well, but all of their contributions are important, and together they would give the team a good start. If these five people can figure out a way to include each person's perspectives and needs, they have a good chance at being an effective team.

This chapter provides a definition of what a team is and examines how type impacts that definition. We identify what different types *expect* from a team and how to develop working agreements to help meet those expectations. We also examine team relationship issues, including the biases people have about one another and how we may reframe those biases. We end with suggestions on how we might analyze teams you are on and what they might need to be more effective.

What Is a Team and How Does Type Impact Teamwork?

A team is two or more people who come together to work on a common goal or task and who need to work together to accomplish that goal most effectively. A team's work includes three major parts:

- the task, or what they're going to do
- the process, or how they're going to do it
- the relationships, or how they're going to interact with each other

In terms of type, the concept of teamwork seems to require behaviors related to Extraversion, Feeling, and Perceiving, as this list of common team tasks illustrates:

Common Team Activities	Associated Type Preferences
Face-to-face meetings	Extraversion
Talking about things	Extraversion
Appreciating the contributions of others	Feeling
Accommodating to the different needs and styles of others	Feeling
Putting group harmony above individual needs	Feeling
Focusing on group process	Feeling
Being flexible	Perceiving
Staying open to others' experiences and ideas	Perceiving

While the concept and definition of teamwork suggest this style, in reality most teams seem to operate more on Thinking and Judging behaviors. Most teams demonstrate these preferences in the following ways:

THINKING

- Making logical decisions
- Focusing on tasks
- Keeping emotions out of the workplace
- Analyzing consequences of different actions

JUDGING

- Structuring everything
- Assigning tasks
- Setting and meeting deadlines
- Planning

Most likely the reason for this behavior is because the values of most organizations emphasize using skills and behaviors associated with Thinking and Judging. In other words, the values of the organization directly influence, in a fairly typical way, what being on a team means.

Type and Our Team

The five people brought together to form our team have different basic expectations, definitions, and needs about teamwork. They each have their own sense of where the team needs to start and their own particular focus. In our example, the primary type influences on expectations of teamwork for the group seem to relate to the preferences for Extraversion and Introversion and for Thinking and Feeling.

The Extraverts, Ted and Joan, may expect that the team will have frequent face-to-face contact and will build on each other's ideas. They probably anticipate that the team will work on things together and people will exchange input and help. The Introverts on the team may, on the other hand, expect that there will be a minimum of meetings, and that they will basically work independently and then come together to report on their progress.

Vivian, like other Feeling types, may assume that joining a team means there will be some connection, camaraderie, shared commitment, and appreciation of each other's contributions. Her focus will likely be on the relationship aspect of the teams and, to a somewhat lesser extent, the process. The rest of the team members prefer Thinking. They may assume that joining the team is primarily a way to get things done; they will expect to divide up tasks and focus on the final product.

Our team members need to make these kinds of expectations known to their colleagues and be willing to collaborate to insure that each team member gets enough of what he or she needs to move forward. Unfortunately, this step, which should be a critical initial phase for any new team, is usually not taken. Frequently people who are joining a team haven't really defined for themselves what they want or expect in a team; therefore, they are not ready to express it to others. This vacuum leaves a lot of room for individual interpretations and misinterpretations.

Effective Teams

In actuality, effective teams need the skills associated with every type preference. We don't mean that a team has to have every type preference represented (in practice, most teams will not), nor should team members be chosen exclusively on the basis of type. Let's remember, teamwork requires that people contribute more than just their type, and preferences don't automatically equal ability and skill in those areas. What we do mean is that for teams to be effective they need to include consciously the tasks, perspectives, and skills associated with each preference.

We've said that teamwork includes "the task." However, we will not address that in this chapter because each team's task is unique, and because it is typically defined by the organization. "The process" includes many pieces covered in other chapters, such as time management, meetings, change, stress, and some additional issues that we will address in the next section. "The relationships" incorporates information from other chapters as well, such as the sections on conflict and stress in Chapters 2, 9, and 10, and some additional issues that we will address in our "Team Relationship Issues" section in this chapter.

Team Process Issues

Teams have ways they typically work together—working agreements—whether the group is aware of them or not. When a group has a history, as a department does, these have usually developed through the years and are informally passed on from employee to employee. When new teams are formed and they include members from different departments, it is particularly important to discuss these working agreements openly. Yet most members of the team typically see their primary job as understanding their task and getting down to business.

By utilizing the concept of type, we can expand working agreements beyond specific tasks to pay attention to interactions among team members and to make these clear and inclusive of all type preferences. When this is not done, the differing definitions and expectations often get teams into trouble.

Team working agreements need to cover the following topics:

What kind of participation do we expect from each other?
How are we going to communicate with each other?
How are we going to make decisions?
Who's going to lead and how?
How will we deal with disagreements and conflicts?
How will we give feedback to one another?
How will we manage our time?
How will we deal with those outside the group?

Reasonable people can hold very different opinions and values on the above topics. Negotiating agreements on these questions can begin the formation of the team. As the team continues its work, the agreements need to be revisited periodically to insure they are working for the group and the individuals.

Type and Working Agreements

The need for working agreements is not type related. However, how people respond to these agreements and what they need/want will differ in part by type. The following come from our experience in using type with teams.

In working agreements, **Extraverts** are likely to want

- frequent verbal communication
- face-to-face interactions that allow exchange of information, problems, and ideas
- decisions that are "talked through," with opportunity to express their views and be heard
- conflicts to be talked through as soon after a disagreement as possible
- frequent, face-to-face, spontaneous feedback that includes opportunity for discussion on differing areas
- to be informed about absences, to be "in the know" about what is going on with people
- to communicate with others outside the group

In working agreements, **Introverts** are likely to want

- written communication, E-mail, or messages
- to work on their own and consult with others as needed
- time to think through a decision
- to avoid and withdraw from disagreements, or at least to deal with them later
- careful written feedback or one-on-one conversations, with an opportunity later to raise additional issues

In working agreements, **Sensors** are likely to want

- communication that is specific and concrete
- full information about issues that are relevant to them (will affect them)
- decision-making to include collection and use of relevant data
- to know who's in charge and how decisions will be made
- to define conflicts clearly and concretely
- to receive feedback about specific behaviors, with general comments about performance to include real examples

In working agreements, **Intuitives** are likely to want

- communication that focuses on the overall plan and general issues, rather than details of everyone's work
- decision-making to include recognition of wider ramifications and consideration of connections
- feedback that assesses overall patterns, with general comments about their impact

In working agreements, **Thinkers** are likely to want

- communication that focuses on tasks and work
- decisions to be based on logic, with assessment of cause and effect and consequences
- leadership that is logical, fair, clear, and consistent
- conflict to be depersonalized and solutions to be focused on what needs to happen for the work to get done

- feedback to focus on their work, their competence, and the task

In working agreements, **Feelers** are likely to want

- communication that includes a personal connection, some recognition of them as an individual
- to be included—to have their opinions solicited and listened to during decision-making
- leadership that is interested in all individuals and sensitive to their varying needs
- support in dealing with conflicts
- recognition that it is difficult for them to focus on the task when personal issues have not been resolved
- feedback to focus on them as an individual—their contributions to the group, their commitment and efforts

In working agreements, **Judging types** are likely to want

- communication that is clear and concise
- decisions to be made quickly, firmly, precisely, and with finality
- leadership that is explicit
- conflict to be resolved or left behind (depending on other preferences)—what they don't like is ambiguity
- an up-front agreement to meet deadlines and follow through, with clear consequences

In working agreements, **Perceiving types** are likely to want

- communication that is wide ranging and includes room for tangents
- decisions to be made only after enough information has been gathered
- opportunities to revisit decisions as needed
- conflict resolution to be a process—they don't like "closing it off" prematurely
- deadlines and structures that are flexible and open to adjustment
- to be trusted to get their work done in a timely way, even if their time frame is different from others

If No Agreements Are in Place

It's easy to see that, in the absence of conscious decisions about working together, team members are likely to assume that others will want what they want. If these issues are not discussed, the assumptions of the organization and type preferences of the majority of the group will take over and become the working agreements. As a result, some perspectives will be ignored, some tasks may not be done, and some individuals may be underutilized.

Team Relationship Issues

Each of us has a natural beginning point—a focus that comes from our type preferences—and we automatically start from that perspective. This provides a filter through which we view everyone. The way we do things (whatever "things" are) seems natural and right, the way things should be done. The tricky part is: *What is true for us—that we are at our best when we approach things from our own perspective—is also true for others: They are at their best when using their own natural approach.* For the team to get the best from each member and to function most effectively, every person's natural style needs to be accepted and utilized at the appropriate times.

Viewing Others from Our Own Perspective: Type Bias

These filters of our own type preferences can become biases that get in the way of accepting and utilizing the perspectives of others. Your central focus can become your type bias and is both a gift and a curse. For example, if detail-oriented David (ISTJ) starts the meeting by giving each team member a copy of his questions and the information he has gathered so far, it is, for him, a natural expression of where he needs to start. Others on the team, however, may have reactions that are rather different from David's intention.

Just-the-big-picture Joan (ENTP), for example, may be thinking: "Why is David asking these questions? They're boring. I have so many exciting ideas for us to discuss. What people have done before is irrelevant because this is all new, and we're certainly not going to let ourselves be limited by the ideas of management. We need to brainstorm the possibilities and move ahead. It's better to ask for forgiveness than permission!"

When unrecognized, type bias can create several issues for teams, including the following:

- the inability to use the valuable contributions of all team members

- getting hung up on the conflict between the team members who always take opposite sides
- disliking and even avoiding working with each other
- distrust of others' intentions

SOME COMMON BIASES BY PREFERENCE

To help you get started in recognizing your own and others' type biases, here are some common ones team members often identify:

- Extraverts may believe Introverts are intentionally withholding information and are uninterested/uninvolved when they are actually thinking about the topic on the inside.

- Introverts may believe Extraverts are superficial and can't stop talking, when Extraverts are simply trying to work out their ideas through conversation and interaction.

- Sensing types may believe Intuitives are unrealistic and too broad in their approach, when Intuitives are focusing on the big picture.

- Intuitives may see Sensing types as picky and negative, as throwing up roadblocks, when they raise practical matters about implementation.

- Thinking types may see Feeling types as taking everything "too personally" and needlessly slowing down the decision-making process when Feeling types are simply insuring that people's individual needs have been considered.

- Feeling types may see Thinking types as critical and uncaring when Thinkers are trying to analyze objectively and make their decisions based on detached logic.

- Judging types may see Perceiving types as lazy or trying to sabotage a project, when Perceivers are not yet ready to move to conclusions.
- Perceiving types may see Judging types as rigid and restrictive, when Judgers are trying to keep tasks on track.

Warning Signs of Type Bias

Here are some warning signs that type bias is in operation:

1. *When people don't recognize the validity and value of ways another type naturally does things;* for example, when Joan (ENTP), who is focused on possibilities, does not recognize the potential contributions of David's (ISTJ) detailed questions.
2. *When people are critical of someone who is acting appropriately and "true" to their type;* for example, Vivian (INFP) reacts negatively to Ted's (ENTJ) appropriately taking charge of structuring the task.
3. *When people value only what they understand, what is natural to them;* for example, if Gail (INTJ) insists that the group can not proceed until they have completely discussed the vision in all its complexity.
4. *When people label opposite preferences as limiting or limited;* for example, group members could react to Joan's (ENTP) exciting possibilities as "fluff" and tangents.
5. *When people attribute motive and intention to opposite preferences, instead of understanding how they function for that person;* for example, Vivian (INFP) could see the Thinking types' focus on task as meaning they do not care about the people issues; and the Thinking types could interpret Vivian's concerns as meaning she does not care about getting the tasks done.

6. *When people find themselves consistently rejecting another viewpoint.* This may show itself if someone in the group frequently says, "I know I've said this before, but. . . ." All of these may indicate you and your team members are operating with some type biases.

REFRAMING TYPE BIASES

Let's look back at our example of detail-oriented David (ISTJ) and just-the-big-picture Joan (ENTP). If Joan is aware of type, conscious of her own starting point and of the fact that others will have different starting points, she could begin with a slightly more positive response than her previous one.

Joan's Biased Thinking	Joan's Reframing
Why is David asking these questions? They're boring. I have so many exciting ideas for us to discuss. What people have done before is irrelevant because this is all new, and we're certainly not going to let ourselves be limited by the ideas of management. We need to brainstorm the possibilities and move ahead. It's better to ask forgiveness than permission!	Who would have thought of that? Is he really interested in those things? I can't even imagine thinking that way. I hate that kind of stuff. But I guess he's got a point. We do need to know some of that background stuff, like what our resources are. If we're going to get this done well in three months we need to use everyone on the team. I just hope we don't get bogged down in the details.

This is an example of reframing. The reality is the same: David is still David and Joan is still Joan. But using an understanding of psychological type allows Joan to listen to David in a different way.

Looking at our team again, here's another example of bias and reframing. If take-charge Ted (ENTJ) starts the meeting by passing out his flow chart of goals and tasks and says, "Our time frame is so tight that we need to get right into this," values-oriented Vivian (INFP), for example, might respond like this:

Vivian's Biased Thinking	Joan's Reframing
Wait a minute—we haven't even talked about how we're going to work together, what roles people will play. We haven't established what people's needs are on the team or for training. Just my luck to be on a team with a steam-roller.	Wow, he has a lot of commitment to getting this project done. It never occurred to me to start with organizational structure and tasks, but I can see we need to pay attention to that if this is going to work. But the people side of this is important too. I'll have to bring up my point of view.

Having examined the instances above, what other type biases can get in the way of this team and your own? How might these be reframed using type knowledge so that the team can work together effectively and make use of each person's potential contributions?

Tips for Dealing with Type Bias

When someone's customary behavior is "driving you up the wall," how can you use your knowledge of type to avoid getting into oppositional impasses? One way to approach this is to ask questions: "David, those are really interesting questions. Can you flesh out for me how they will help us on this project?" Understand that the other's motive and potential contributions to the team's work are usually very helpful.

The following is a brief summary of the typical central motivation or focus of each type and the contributions they will likely bring to teamwork. Keeping these in mind during interactions can help you reframe your own natural type biases.

CENTRAL MOTIVATORS FOR EACH TYPE

ISTJ	ISFJ	INFJ	INTJ
Collect, select, and use relevant data	Draw on their experience to make things go smoothly for people	Encourage personal growth of members to achieve their vision	Provide long-term strategic vision
ISTP	**ISFP**	**INFP**	**INTP**
Deal with the realities in a logical way	Provide behind-the-scenes loyal support for their team members	Keep the group true to its mission and values	Give clear, logical analyses of core issues and tasks
ESTP	**ESFP**	**ENFP**	**ENTP**
Solve problems on the spot	Involve everyone and make it fun	See the team's potential and enthusiastically encourage its growth	Constantly bring new ideas and possibilities to the team
ESTJ	**ESFJ**	**ENFJ**	**ENTJ**
Organize the tasks and get them done	Search for and find ways to take care of the people around them	Facilitate the participation of everyone in the team	Take charge and provide strategic direction

Understanding these motivations can be the starting point for your reframing process. Working to understand them and their potential contributions can help move teams from being irritated by their types to taking advantage of the type differences.

Analyzing Your Team

As you can see from the above, if you were fortunate enough to have all sixteen types on a team, your team would be whole. It would have everything it needs to work effectively, assuming it includes the task expertise. Teams, in our experience, rarely have all sixteen types, even when they are large, but they can take advantage of all the preferences in their work by taking the time to apply some of the knowledge about type to their team.

If You Know the Types on Your Team

Here are the steps:

1. *List your team members' types and then count how many of each preference you have.* For example, with our newly formed team we have:

2 Extraverts	3 Introverts
1 Sensor	4 Intuitives
4 Thinkers	1 Feeler
3 Judging types	2 Perceiving types

This team has all the preferences, although not in equal numbers.

2. *Examine the ways the team's preferences may affect your work. If the team has balance* (nearly equal numbers on a particular preference dimension), as our team does on E-I and J-P, this can lead to a healthy use of each preference to balance the group's perspectives and work. However, it can also lead to

a destructive tug-of-war within the team. Such a team may have people of opposite preferences continually misunderstanding one another or balancing each other and constructively using their differences.

If the team is imbalanced in a particular preference dimension, as our team is on S-N and T-F, consider what the team may be missing. For example, because of the S-N imbalance (just one Sensing type), our present team may need to be particularly careful that they consider the realities, the relevant experiences, the steps needed to design and implement the new program, and so on.

Because of the T-F imbalance (only one Feeling type), they may need to insure that they give proper weight to the importance of group interactions, include the viewpoints of people outside the group, and recognize the impact of their decisions on others.

In an ideal team, David and Vivian (our lone S and F types) would insist on their contributions being included, but in fact, this is very difficult in the real world. They will need the support of the majority members to make this happen and may need invitations to contribute.

When there is significant imbalance, the majority may not hear minority concerns or may dismiss them as irrelevant. Minority people can feel like a "voice in the wilderness" when they see issues clearly and no one is listening to them. It is crucial that the team recognizes this issue and devises explicit ways to solicit the views of the minority or the missing pieces and make them a part of their regular functioning.

3. *Identify the leader's type and the potential impact on the team.* Team leaders need to be aware of the impact of their type on the team. Their strengths (and limitations) are likely to be magnified in their leadership role. They may have to make spe-

cial efforts to communicate with and include team members whose preferences are different from their own.

For example, Introverted leaders will need to be sure that the Extraverts on their team are getting enough information, talk time, and feedback; this will take extra energy. Conversely, Extraverted leaders need to be careful not to interrupt others, not to expect active participation at meetings from the Introverts, and to give them time to reflect.

4. *Initiate ways to deal with the issues you have identified. Ask people who have a minority preference, "What are we missing?"* For example, our team might say, "Vivian, what are we overlooking? Can you suggest some ways we can include that?" The group then needs to follow through on the suggestions, and check back with the minority person to insure the suggestions have been implemented appropriately.

If a type preference is totally absent from a group, the group must generate that perspective. Thus, if there are no Perceiving types, they can ask, "What would a Perceiving preference be asking right now?" They might come up with questions such as the following: "Is there more information we need? Is there one more way of looking at this? Have we considered all the relevant options before deciding?" (See "Effective Decision-Making" section in Chapter 5 for suggested questions.)

With both minority and missing preferences, a team can go outside and check out their assumptions and decisions with people of different preferences. Your group can also use the questions to aid decision-making in Chapter 5 and the descriptions of the motivators of the sixteen types as a structure for discussing these questions. In time such questions can become almost automatic. A team can just learn to ask itself, "Have we covered all the bases?"

If your team has people of opposite types continually mis-

understanding one another, perhaps those on the team who share several letters in common with each can help bridge the differences. For example, if an ESTJ and INFP are always on opposite sides, perhaps an ENFJ teammate can help bring them together.

Using Type Knowledge When You Don't Know People's Types

When you don't know team members' types, you can't predict very accurately what the team may be missing, but you can be sure that your team decisions will be better if you've included all the perspectives. Use the above approaches to help you include the different perspectives. This may also help you avoid major costly errors, for it acts as a final check that you have covered all the bases. If you're in a team setting where using your knowledge of type is not appropriate or possible, you can still make a contribution by asking the questions, even without reference to type. Your own knowledge will then provide balance to the team.

Teams That Work

When a team works together well, people have inspirational, even landmark, experiences. Whether the team is gathered for work, sports, a political campaign, or to change the public schools, members recall a successful team effort as a high point in their lives. The whole was greater than the sum of the parts, and the members retain warm feelings about others on the team, whether they liked them on a personal level or not. They remember themselves as being effective, having high energy, and simply working at their best.

Yet today, when the workplace is full of teams, many people find teamwork frustrating and difficult. They make comments like, "It would be easier to just do it myself" or "If I hear about teamwork one more time, I'll scream." When teams **don't** work, they provide lasting memories of frustration, continuing anger toward team members who were difficult, and personal feelings of incompetence.

All the things we suggest in this chapter are likely to make teamwork take longer, at least in the formation stage. Studies of teams[1] have found that, when teams have a variety of type perspectives, it does take longer to communicate effectively and work together, but the outcome is of a higher quality. Teams with more similar types find themselves communicating more easily, but are more likely to have "blind spots" or things they overlook in their work.

Revisiting Our Team

If our team utilized the suggestions found in this chapter, they would work more effectively and enjoy their time together. This positive outcome would be illustrated in the following ways:

1. They would have an excellent product.
   - The training program would have met the needs of both the organization and the employees.
   - It would have been "doable" and smoothly implemented.
2. The process, or how they did the work, would have made use of their individual type differences.

- Their working agreements would have made it possible for everyone to contribute.
- They would have learned the value of different perspectives and continued to seek those out.
- They would have learned to look outside *and* inside for ideas and data.

3. The group would have developed relationships of mutual respect.
   - They would have learned to reframe their type biases.
   - They would rely on each other in their future work.

The long-term benefits for each individual on the team may also then include personal growth and development.

Tips for Teamwork

1. Start with yourself.
   - What do you like to contribute?
   - What are your type biases?
2. Since teamwork requires some compromise, identify your real priorities.
   - What's most important to you?
   - What are you willing to negotiate?
3. Help your team carve out working agreements.
4. As problems occur, continue using your knowledge of type to identify sources of and solutions to problems.
5. Apply type not just to relationship issues, but also to problem-solving issues to make sure you've covered all the bases.
6. Laugh at your differences instead of being annoyed by them.

CHAPTER 7

EXPLORING ANOTHER LEVEL OF TYPE

here is more to psychological type than just the four preferences or even the information that comes from looking at two preferences together. Each of the preferences influences the way a person will express the others—it's a dynamic interaction. ESTJs do not Extravert in the same ways that ENFPs Extravert; the other three preferences influence the content and expression of the Extraversion that the two types share. ENFPs and INFPs, who are different in only one type preference, are very different in what they rely on and use most. This dynamic picture includes several important ideas that can expand our understanding of our own and others' functioning in important ways: the need for balance in our personalities, the importance of a well-developed core identity, and an innate drive for growth.

The Importance of Balance

Carl Jung, who developed the theory on which the MBTI is based, emphasized the need for balance in order for human beings to be effective in work and relationships. This necessary balance, in terms of type, takes several different forms: between Extraverting and Introverting and between gathering information and making decisions. The discussion below explains some of the theory upon which "type dynamics" is based.

Balance between Extraverting and Introverting

Every person needs to be able to Extravert (to deal with the external world, to express ideas and perspectives, to interact with others) and to be able to Introvert (to be in touch with the internal world of memories, ideas, and emotions; to reflect). When Extraverts are too involved and busy in the outside world, they need to turn inward to reflect and gain some equilibrium. When Introverts are too engaged in internal reflection, in figuring things out, they need to turn outward to express those thoughts and get others' ideas.

The dynamics of type suggest that each of the sixteen types contains an Extraverted and an Introverted aspect, whatever their first letter. For information about your own type's Extraverted and Introverted parts, see the table on page 156.

Balance between Gathering Information and Making Decisions

Every person also needs some balance between taking in information (whether by Sensing or Intuition) and making decisions (whether by Thinking or Feeling). If we spent all our time taking in information without applying any decision-making, we would never prioritize or structure that information to decide upon and commit ourselves to a course of action. If we used only our decision-making component, we would make snap decisions perhaps based on prejudice, rather than making informed ones. For effective functioning, we need trustworthy processes for carrying out both of these activities.

What Happens When We Don't Have Balance?

No one is, or can be, perfectly balanced. In Jung's theory and the MBTI, balance does not mean spending equal time Extraverting and Introverting, nor being able to do both equally well. And the same is true of the other preference dimensions: One end of each will be more preferred, developed, and used. Balance, in terms of type, means being able to Extravert and Introvert when appropriate, and having both a reliable way to gather information and to make decisions. It also means gaining access to our nonpreferred parts—recognizing their value and finding ways to use them when it's appropriate and necessary.

The Importance of the Favorite Function: A Type's Core Identity

The dynamic picture of personality painted by Jung and Myers and Briggs also includes recognition that each type has a favorite part, one mental function (Sensing, Intuition, Thinking, or Feeling) that forms the core of our identity and the focus of our personality. In each of the sixteen types, that favorite part will be one of the two middle letters. Myers and Briggs devised a formula for determining which function (or middle letter) was the favorite. While this seems rather arbitrary, their ideas were based on years of observation as well as on Jung's theory.

The interested reader is referred to the Notes for further reading on this.[1, 2, 3]

For Extraverts, this favorite part will be the middle letter that they Extravert (remember, each type will Extravert one of the two middle letters and each type will Introvert one). Introverts will Introvert the middle letter that is their favorite. This is because we use our favorite, core part in the world that we most prefer to be in. To find your favorite part, and indeed the order of all your preferences, see the table on page 156.

For most people, this favorite part, which is usually referred to as "the dominant function," is the one they developed first, as a child. It's the part that feels most reliable and trustworthy, most comfortable, most like themselves. They continue to go to it first and most often. Let's look at a couple of similar types to see how this theory of a dominant function works.

> ESFJs' favorite, most important part is Extraverted Feeling. Their second favorite is Introverted Sensing (remember the balance between the outside Extraversion and the inside Introversion!). This means that gathering specific, detailed, and complete information (Introverted Sensing) is important to them, but their primary focus is on creating a friendly, harmonious climate in their immediate environment (Extraverted Feeling). If the two come into conflict, creating harmony and goodwill with those around them will win out.

> ISFJs' favorite, most important part is Introverted Sensing. Their second favorite is Extraverted Feeling (again, the balance). Being aware of and responsive to the needs of those in their immediate environment (Extraverted Feeling) is important to them, but their primary focus is making decisions that fit with their internally stored, specific information about how things have been and should be

done (Introverted Sensing). If the two come into conflict, relying on their internal knowledge of how things are and should be will win out.

The Favorite Functions of Each Type

There are eight different dominant functions among the sixteen types:

- **Introverted Sensing (shared by ISTJs and ISFJs)**
  Relying on a wealth of internally stored, specific data
- **Extraverted Sensing (shared by ESTPs and ESFPs)**
  Experiencing the present moment and seeking new experiences
- **Introverted Intuition (shared by INFJs and INTJs)**
  Forming complex inner pictures of the world and the future
- **Extraverted Intuition (shared by ENTPs and ENFPs)**
  Scanning the environment for new ideas, possibilities, and patterns
- **Introverted Thinking (shared by INTPs and ISTPs)**
  Forming internal logical explanations
- **Extraverted Thinking (shared by ESTJs and ENTJs)**
  Organizing their external environment by logical principles
- **Introverted Feeling (shared by ISFPs and INFPs)**
  Filtering everything through their internal values
- **Extraverted Feeling (shared by ESFJs and ENFJs)**
  Structuring the external environment to achieve harmony

In each pair above, the two types share the dominant (or favorite) function but have a different "second favorite," or auxiliary, balancing function. The table below shows what those are for each type as well as the order of the other two functions.

Order of Preferences for Each Type[4]

ISTJ	ISFJ	INFJ	INTJ
1. Sensing (I)	1. Sensing (I)	1. Intuition (I)	1. Intuition (I)
2. Thinking (E)	2. Feeling (E)	2. Feeling (E)	2. Thinking (E)
3. Feeling (E or I)	3. Thinking (E or I)	3. Thinking (E or I)	3. Feeling (E or I)
4. Intuition (E)	4. Intuition (E)	4. Sensing (E)	4. Sensing (E)
ISTP	**ISFP**	**INFP**	**INTP**
1. Thinking (I)	1. Feeling (I)	1. Feeling (I)	1. Thinking (I)
2. Sensing (E)	2. Sensing (E)	2. Intuition (I)	2. Intuition (E)
3. Intuition (E or I)	3. Intuition (E or I)	3. Sensing (E or I)	3. Sensing (E or I)
4. Feeling (E)	4. Thinking (E)	4. Thinking (E)	4. Feeling (E)
ESTP	**ESFP**	**ENFP**	**ENTP**
1. Sensing (E)	1. Sensing (E)	1. Intuition (E)	1. Intuition (E)
2. Thinking (I)	2. Feeling (I)	2. Feeling (I)	2. Thinking (I)
3. Feeling (E or I)	3. Thinking (E or I)	3. Thinking (E or I)	3. Feeling (E or I)
4. Intuition (I)	4. Intuition (I)	4. Sensing (I)	4. Sensing (I)
ESTJ	**ESFJ**	**ENFJ**	**ENTJ**
1. Thinking (E)	1. Feeling (E)	1. Feeling (E)	1. Thinking (E)
2. Sensing (I)	2. Sensing (I)	2. Intuition (E)	2. Intuition (I)
3. Intuition (E or I)	3. Intuition (E or I)	3. Sensing (E or I)	3. Sensing (E or I)
4. Feeling (I)	4. Thinking (I)	4. Thinking (I)	4. Feeling (I)

Remember that E means this function is expressed mainly in the Extraverted, or outside, world, and that I means this function is expressed mainly in the Introverted, or inside, world.

What Do These Eight Favorite Functions Look Like in Action?

Let's take a look at an activity that is (or should be!) a regular part of work life: having a celebration. This might involve recognizing a department or team that met its goals, celebrating a new contract, or commemorating a success or another important event from the past. Each of the favorite functions would be likely to approach such a task differently, to ask different questions and offer different perspectives.

Planning a work celebration

Introverted Sensing (ISTJ & ISFJ) (Relying on a wealth of specific, internally stored data): What have we done in the past? What are the company policies about these celebrations? Does the company insurance policy cover it? When, where, who's invited, how much money will it cost? Who will do the invitations and a map?

Extraverted Sensing (ESTP & ESFP) (Experiencing the present moment and seeking new experiences): What have we done before that was fun? What activities will we have? Let's check out different sites. What do we wear?

Introverted Intuition (INFJ & INTJ) (Forming complex inner pictures of the world and the future): Let me develop an internal picture of the celebration and how it fits who we are as a company.

Extraverted Intuition (ENFP & ENTP) (Scanning for new ideas, possibilities, and patterns): Let's generate possibilities that are unique and outrageous. How about the zoo or the symphony or renting a double-decker bus or . . . ?

Introverted Thinking (ISTP & INTP) (Forming internal logical explanations): Why a party? What's the purpose? Justification? What are the components of a successful celebration?

Extraverted Thinking (ESTJ & ENTJ) (Organizing their external environment by logical principles): First let's define the purpose. Identify steps we'll take to get the celebration going. Time frame? Who does what? What's the agenda of the celebration?

Introverted Feeling (ISFP & INFP) (Filtering everything through their internal values): How will it reflect our company values? Will it be authentic and meaningful?

Extraverted Feeling (ESFJ & ENFJ) (Structuring the external environment to achieve harmony): Who will be invited? Let's create the right ambience. What will please everyone? Let's have special things for each person to do.

As we look at the favorite functions in action another point is illustrated: Each dominant function brings value to any task, whether it's celebrating, planning a project, creating a new product, dealing with customers, or keeping the business running daily.

Cautions of Sterotyping

When people first learn about type and the MBTI, they sometimes think, "This is great. Now we can see that our customer-service people should all be *SF*s." This can lead to inappropriate uses of type: stereotyping, pigeonholing, or limiting people. There are many approaches to customer service, not just an SF one. Each type brings a particular set of strengths to any task. While *SF*s may naturally relate well to individuals, other type combinations can make different contributions.

*ST*s can help customers identify relevant data and specific uses.

*NF*s can support customers in trusting their own sense of their needs.

*NT*s can help customers develop a depth of knowledge about the product.

And not all *SF*s want to direct their talents to customer service!

Type dynamics and recognizing the contributions of each of the dominant functions can help move us toward the deeper understanding available from type: Everyone has important strengths and contributions; everyone has blind spots and weaknesses. Every human activity will be improved by involving people with different perspectives in a real way, by having them involved throughout the process. Such knowledge can lead us toward the constructive use of differences. It can also provide guidance for our individual developmental paths.

Balancing the Dominant Function

Each type presents its own challenges in developing balance and in using its dominant function effectively. The following are some of the most common ones:

EJs (ESTJ, ESFJ, ENFJ, AND ENTJ)

These four types may find themselves moving quickly toward decisions and expressing their opinions freely. Others may experience *EJ*s as controlling or see them as opinionated.

They may need to work on balancing this decisiveness by spending more time gathering information and considering its implications before deciding.

EPs (ESTP, ESFP, ENFP, AND ENTP)

These four types may find themselves gathering lots of information and enjoying the search for new possibilities or data. Taking risks is fun. They may rush to try out things before having analyzed them thoroughly. Others may see them as impulsive, unfocused, and changeable.

They may need to work on balancing this data gathering by spending more time deciding what's most important and what's the best direction to take in order to provide an anchor for their exploration.

IPs (ISTP, ISFP, INFP, AND INTP)

These four types may find themselves appearing to others as flexible since they consider a lot of information, but in things they care about they move firmly toward internal decisions. Others may not understand how they came to their decisions and decided what's really important.

They may need to work on communicating the inner principles and values that guide them, their internal processes for making decisions.

IJs (ISTJ, ISFJ, INFJ, AND INTJ)

These four types may appear decisive and organized to others, but inside they are gathering information and delaying decisions until that internal information base seems clear and complete to them. Others do not see the information behind the decision, and may be puzzled by delays in decisions or see them as overly cautious.

They may need to work on ways to communicate their internal information or pictures and on taking some risks and making some decisions before information is complete and perfect.

Recognizing the value of balance, the power of the dominant function, and our own dynamic functioning can assist each of us in identifying ways in which we're likely to be effective as well as where we may not be as effective as we could be. This is the first step leading us to appreciating the contributions of others and in identifying areas for our own developmental activities. Below we discuss type development.

Type Development

This deeper level of understanding also suggests that each type has a likely pattern of development. Of course, each person has a unique developmental path based on individual experience such as family, cultural values, education, and so on. Nevertheless, the model of type development presented by Jung and Myers and Briggs can provide a tool for looking at and assessing the individual path.

All of the preferences have value and, in fact, we all use them at least part of the time:

- We all notice, collect, and store specific, realistic information (Sensing).
- We all make connections between facts and see meanings (Intuition).
- Everyone applies logic to assess the pros and cons in making decisions (Thinking).
- Everyone considers the impact on people and uses values in making decisions (Feeling).

All these processes are normal human activities, and all have contributions to make—but most of us don't manage all of them equally well.

Type development helps explain why we do some of these better than others and also identifies potentialities each of us has for the future.

The Favorite Function in Childhood

Most people develop their favorite (dominant) function during childhood.

An **Introverted Sensing child (ISTJ or ISFJ)** may be attracted to "real life" play: school, going to work, etc. They put energy into learning "the rules" and getting a solid sense of what is expected (IS).

An **Extraverted Sensing child (ESTP or ESFP)** may actively seek new experiences and people, reveling in enjoyment of activities, such as field trips and experiential learning, exploring the world around him/her just to experience it (ES).

An **Introverted Intuitive child (INFJ or INTJ)** may spend a lot of time "daydreaming," creating internal images and pictures of the future (IN).

An **Extraverted Intuitive child (ENFP or ENTP)** may lead his or her contemporaries in creative play like getting everyone involved in "make believe" games (EN).

An **Introverted Thinking child (ISTP or INTP)** may spend a lot of time trying to "figure things out," reading an encyclopedia, learning about the stars, taking in and organizing knowledge (IT).

An **Extraverted Thinking child (ESTJ or ENTJ)** may try to organize and structure the world around him/her by planning family outings, organizing school activities, or providing leadership to a social group (ET).

An **Introverted Feeling child (ISFP or INFP)** may be especially sensitive to those around him or her, quietly noticing how others are treated, identifying with outsiders, speaking up fiercely when his/her values are violated (IF).

An **Extraverted Feeling child (ESFJ or ENFJ)** may focus on ensuring that everyone around him/her is included and feels counted, staying after school to help the teacher, organizing family chores and outings (EF).

In each of these cases, the child *puts* time and energy into experiencing the favorite function and *gets* energy from engaging in such activities.

Because of the energy, time, and attention this favorite function receives, it typically becomes very well developed, reliable, and a central part of that child's self-identity. Though other parts are likely to receive energy and to develop later in life, the favorite function remains the core of the personality.

Of course there are exceptions. Sometimes children who prefer Introversion seem to put more energy into the second-favorite, auxiliary part—the one that they Extravert. Parents or the culture may encourage and support Extraverted behaviors such as sociability and playing with others, which may mean the Introverted dominant function doesn't receive much time or energy.

Balance Provided by the Second Favorite

At some point, people also direct energy toward the second-favorite part (their auxiliary function), the one that can provide important balance. For a person whose favorite part is one of the perceiving functions (Sensing or Intuition), this second-favorite part will be their preferred judging function (Thinking or Feeling), and vice versa. The development of this second part gives the personality reliable ways to take in information and to make decisions, which are necessary components for successful living.

The second-favorite part will also be used to interact with the less preferred world. That is, because the dominant function is used in the favorite world (whether external or internal), the auxiliary function will be used in the other world to provide balance. Extraverts will then be developing their Introverted part, while Introverts are developing a more Extraverted part.

This developmental model, then, pictures adults as usually

having developed a central core identity and balance in their functioning.

The Impact of Environment

Many people have not been totally supported in the development of their preferences. Sometimes family or school expected and required them to act differently. Work requirements can also interfere with a smooth path of development.

An ENTP girl, for example, may not have found support for her favorite childhood activity of creating imaginative games and involving others in interesting activities. As an adolescent, her developing logic and critical analysis may have "turned off" her peers and others, who saw this as not feminine. If she ends up in accounting, and starts work doing the routine, everyday tasks that require concentration and exactitude, she probably won't find support for her preferences there either.

Such environmental influences can lead to development of skills in nonpreferred areas. That can be very helpful, but it can also be tiring, interfere with development of the preferred areas, and lead to problems in self-confidence and a secure sense of identity.

Midlife and Beyond

At midlife (which comes at different ages for different people), some significant energy shifts occur for most people. This is the time when people look at their life as it has been and ask themselves, "Is this all there is?" It's a time when people question the decisions they've made in the past, find themselves drawn to different possibilities, and begin to see potentials in areas that before they might have found uninteresting.

Midlife, then, can be the beginning of new development possibilities. It can be the gateway to continued growth and development throughout the life span.

An ESTJ, for example, may have focused in her twenties and thirties on being a super administrator, planning for efficient setting and achieving of goals, making things run smoothly and on schedule (ST). Then, in her forties, she may find herself more interested in the larger meanings and connections of her work and in people relationships (NF).

Such shifts in energy do not mean that she has changed her type preferences. Instead, she is expanding her awareness and finding new options for herself. Others may experience it as a "softening" of her personality, but they will usually still see the clear ESTJ logical structure! She will often pursue her development in ESTJ ways, for example, by volunteering for committees to help benefit her community or by taking a class in developing people skills or in creative problem-solving and "out of the box" thinking (all of which are logical, specific learning activities).

Using Type Dynamics and Development at Work

These deeper levels of type knowledge open up new ways to use type knowledge at work. They can help us understand who we are at a deeper level and provide guidance for developmental activities. They can assist us in developing our own decision-making processes to be more balanced and effective.

They can help us understand others better. Recognizing that others have an Introverted part (even the Extraverts) can expand our understanding of how others function and help explain their sometimes puzzling behavior.

The following three chapters—on dealing with organizational change, stress, and developing yourself at work—all draw on these deeper levels of type. They will illustrate some of the concepts we've discussed in this chapter and also show some of the usefulness of dynamics and development.

CHAPTER 8

CHANGE

A Change Is About to Take Place

Cast of characters:
Leader, ENTP
Executive council, ENTJs and INTJs
Jean, ESTJ
Paul, ESFJ
Nancy, ENFP
Tony, ISTJ
Linda, INTP

arren Products, Inc., calls a company-wide meeting to announce another organizational change.

Leader (ENTP): "We are announcing a new initiative, XYZ. The executive council has studied various options and decided this is the way Warren Products needs to go.

"Here are the plan, the schedule, and the training sessions to teach everyone to work in this new system. It's going to take a great deal of work and commitment from everyone.

"I'm excited about the plan: It gives us an opportunity to position ourselves to meet the challenges of the future. I know you'll all get on board and make this work."

A group of employees who work together as a team goes to lunch after the meeting and discusses the leader's presentation:

Jean (ESTJ): "Another one of those stupid changes. Can you believe it? Remember when they announced the restructuring a year ago? It just hasn't worked. We couldn't even figure out how to route our mail for the first three months, and people still don't know who to call. And we sure haven't seen all the savings they promised."

Paul (ESFJ): "XYZ is going to be so hard on everyone. People are going to be so upset. Is this going to affect our salaries? I can feel my stomach tightening up already."

Nancy (ENFP): "Well, now wait a minute. Just because the restructuring hasn't worked well, it doesn't mean this can't. I can see some real exciting possibilities here."

Tony (ISTJ): "I'm feeling really confused. What exactly are we supposed to do? What's going to happen to our department? How are we going to meet our customers' needs and keep our regular work going? This will be so much work! We've already got too much to do."

Jean: "I agree."

Paul: "Oh, Tony, you know your job. I know you're worried about keeping up with all your work, but you're so good at what you do, you'll be able to handle it. We know we can always count on you."

Nancy: "That's right. We're a really competent group of people here. We can handle this. Give it a chance."

*Jean: "Yes, **we're** competent, but I'm not sure **they** are."*

Tony: "And I don't have time to do all this new stuff! They're going to give us these so-called great ideas and then leave it to us to figure out how to do them, as usual. It's just too much."

Paul: "Linda, you're very quiet. What do you think about this?"

Linda (INTP): "Look, I don't think we can tell anything at this point. Let's not get too excited or worried about it. They will probably change their mind again next week, and it won't ever even happen. We can worry about what we need to do when we actually see something happening."

Jean: "Mark my words: There are going to be problems, no matter what happens!"

Current Models of Change

Most models for organizational change lay out the process in clear, understandable steps, including what's needed from vision to completion. These are good models. They say the right things. The problem: They overlook individual differences and the impact those differences have on implementation of the model.

Many of the models for change see change as:

- Transformational: they're not incremental or step-by-step modifications; examples of transformational models include reengineering the corporation, creating the ideal organization, zero-based planning.

- Inspirational: depend on motivating people with an inspiring vision of the future that everyone should be able to see.

- Fast-paced: they're impatient with those of us who move at a different pace.

- Systems-oriented: just change the system and the people will adjust.

- Technical more than personal: change is separate from emotions.

- Good: after all, doing the same things in the same ways is bad!

These pictures of change require individual initiative and independence. Just give us the big picture and we'll go with it, no problem! Everyone should be motivated to change. It's exciting!

Most plans for change have an ENTP perspective. (ENTPs generate ideas, are systems-oriented, and very independent. They think people ought to be able to adjust and are impatient with those who do not move as quickly.) Looking at this through type filters, it becomes clear that most change plans are missing some pieces that are important for other types. These filters help explain some of what is seen as resistance to change. In actuality, it may not be because people hate any change or even because they don't like that particular change. It may be that they have not gotten the information they need to understand the desired change or that the plan does not include what they need to implement the change.

Of course, even ENTPs can struggle with change when it is imposed on them. Everyone expresses difficulty with imposed change when they have had little say and are just expected to implement. Ideally, people would like to be involved in the process of deciding on changes. In reality, it is usually up to the individual to figure out how to move from being a passive recipient of plans for change to being an active participant in the process. And quite frankly, that may not always be possible.

The current reality and foreseeable future involve constant change. People's first response may be to want to avoid the change and to hope it will go away, but our experience is that every organization is involved in significant change. It can't be escaped. Most organizations provide some, but seldom all, of what individuals need to deal successfully with the changes.

The Change Process for Individuals

The biggest question for the individual employee in the current environment of organizational change is, **What can I do to feel satisfied and successful, to feel that I am contributing something worthwhile while change goes on all around me?**

We suggest the following steps to help in developing your own vision of the future and finding your place in it:

1. Gather information, including the reasons for change.
2. Recognize the role of the past.
3. Decide specifically what needs to be changed.
4. Identify what you need in order to make the changes, including how you can get the necessary resources within your current environment.

1. Reasons for the Change

There are many reasons—external and internal—underlying current organizational change. Developing an understanding of the factors impacting your organization will give you the background you need to begin assessing what changes are needed and why.

The information you gather may be data about your organization's current financial performance and threats to its continuing existence. It could be information about the opportunity to fill a new niche. It can include the big picture, what's going on in your industry or in society that is affecting your company.

At this stage of gathering information, psychological type

plays an important role: It assists people in identifying the kinds of information they will find most helpful and persuasive, and the approach to gathering data that will work best for them. We have found that focusing on the needs of people's favorite or dominant process can assist them in recognizing what they need in order to prepare themselves to understand, and perhaps influence, proposed changes.

Those whose most important process is **Sensing (ISTJ, ISFJ, ESTP, ESFP)** usually share the following information-gathering style:

- focus on what's real and actual: who, what, when, where, why
- notice practical data, data that can be put to use in the present situation; if they cannot see how it applies, they are not as interested
- focus on present realities or past experience; the future is not real—it's all projection, guesswork
- focus on the pieces, parts, and steps; want to gather the full range of specific information available, fill in any gaps, and resolve any contradictory information before making decisions

The Introverts here (ISTJ and ISFJ) will feel most completely informed and ready for making decisions if they are given access to the kinds of information they seek (see above) and given enough time to pursue, collect, and refine it. Don't surprise them!

The Extraverts in this group (ESTP and ESFP) want to be active with others in collecting data and rely on trial and error in the information-gathering process. They want to try out different approaches, seek out different people's knowledge and experience, and allow the decisions to come out of this process.

For all those whose favorite process is Sensing, the gathering of the realistic, practical data is crucial to developing their understanding of the present situation, exploring the options for future change, and becoming part of the change.

Those whose most important process is **Intuition (INFJ, INTJ, ENFP, ENTP)** usually share the following information-gathering style:

- focus on big-picture possibilities; see crises as challenges, as opportunities for creative solutions
- pay attention to imaginative insights; trust insight more than experience or specific data about the present
- want information that they can connect to other ideas; the broad outlines or trends are easiest to connect
- find meaning in the patterns and connections; search for meaning in data, ignore data that doesn't fit

The Introverts here (INFJ and INTJ) want to get a little information from others and then have time to take it inside and see how it connects to their sense of the situation and the future. Their own internal picture and how the present fits with it are most important to them. They do not want decisions to be made until all becomes clear to them.

The Extraverts included (ENFP and ENTP) want to brainstorm possibilities with others, consult with people they know who may have some interesting perspectives, and bring in information they have from other sources (books they have read, ideas they have heard about). They may want to begin experimenting with various alternatives while pursuing a number of options at the same time, and the final decisions will not be made until every possible option is explored.

For all those whose favorite process is Intuition, gathering the "big picture" information is crucial to their understanding the current situation and positioning themselves to participate in the changes.

Those whose favorite process is Thinking or Feeling tend to shape the way they collect data by the structure, values, and principles that are most important to their favorite process. Typically, they will feel more comfortable gathering less data before making decisions than those whose favorite process is Sensing or Intuition who are described above. This is especially true for those who prefer E and J, and therefore use their decision-making in the external world.

Those whose most important process is **Thinking (ISTP, INTP, ESTJ, ENTJ)** are likely to approach information gathering from the following perspective:

- look for impersonal, objective data, who's right and who's wrong; research, verify, seek supporting evidence
- seek cause and effect; ask the "why" questions
- want to frame the data for ready analysis; what are the pros and cons?
- focus on gathering information to solve problems with logic; data needs to fit into their logical system or be persuasive enough to redo their logical system
- disdain information that is not logical, regardless of who presents it

The Introverts here (ISTP and INTP) want to find the structure in the data. They process and structure data as it comes in, designing an internal system for understanding it.

For the Extraverts in this group (ESTJ and ENTJ), decision and action are more important than gathering data. They want to decide on solutions quickly, set up goals, design the implementation, and get things moving.

Those whose most important process is **Feeling (ISFP, INFP, ESFJ, ENFJ)** are likely to approach information gathering from the following perspective:

- look for information connected to their personal values and experience; find out the experience and opinions of the people who are important to them
- want to know how others feel about it and to share how they feel about it; need to process information with others and talk about it
- want to assess information by how it affects individuals
- try to identify the common experiences, the things that people share; want to find ways to bring people together, to form consensus for decisions
- ignore or are uninterested in impersonal, especially statistical data

The Introverts here (ISFP and INFP) focus on their internal value system and gather information related to those values. They want to know how their values can be supported in the current environment.

The Extraverts (ESFJ and ENFJ) in this group focus on the needs of others and their own valuing of and need for harmony in their external environment. They scan for information that will allow everyone to feel good, that can lead to "win-win" decisions.

Now focus on yourself. How do you like to gather information? What information would help you understand some of the current changes in your organization?

People's types, as you can see, lead them to see different reasons for change, all of which are valid.

2. The Role of the Past

Type leads people to value the past in different ways, as well. An organization's identity and traditions are important factors in deciding on changes and figuring out how to implement them in productive and effective ways. Plans and policies that will work in one organization may be disastrous failures in another with a different history and culture.

Taking stock of the past—significant people, events, and emotions—may help individuals handle change. Personality preferences play a part in what people recall and value in the past. They may find this recollection valuable because it

- validates the history and experience of the group or organization;
- helps people see the big picture;
- highlights trends, providing metaphors for understanding;
- values people's experience;
- explains relationships.

Those preferring **Sensing and Thinking (ISTJ, ISTP, ESTP, ESTJ)** find exploring the past useful because:

- They want people to hear about it and to count it in decisions about the future.
- They want to build on it, include it in formulating the future vision and the changes.
- They respect facts: who, what, when, where, why?
- It provides a kind of objective scorecard: what worked, what didn't—it's "real" data.

Looking at the past assures *ST*s that everyone has heard, understood, and recognized the group's experience.

Those preferring **Sensing and Feeling (ISFJ, ISFP, ESFP, ESFJ)** find exploring the past useful for most of the reasons *ST*s give, and for some additional reasons of their own:

- It includes the relationships—it gives the facts with feeling.
- It allows them to see and feel good about the role they personally have played.
- It remembers and validates their relationships, the people who have been important to them.
- It affirms their sense of belonging, of being an important part of the group.
- It helps others see why doing things a certain way is so important to them.
- It identifies some of the losses they have experienced.

Looking at the past assures *SF*s that their personal memories will not be lost, that the past is appreciated and valued.

Those preferring **Intuition and Feeling (INFJ, INFP, ENFP, ENFJ)** find exploring the past useful because:

- It helps them see the big picture.

- It provides metaphors for understanding (surviving in our organization is like running a marathon).
- They can identify trends.
- It explains relationships between people, departments, and ideas.
- It gives them ideas about the group and helps them understand the group better; it helps them understand their place and role in the group and its history.

Looking at the past helps *NF*s see how to move the group toward consensus and how to help the group move forward together.

Those preferring **Intuition and Thinking (INTJ, INTP, ENTP, ENTJ)** find exploring the past useful because:

- It illuminates the big picture.
- They can identify trends and patterns that explain the past, present, and future to them.
- It provides a conceptual framework to put people into; "Now I understand."
- They can make connections to things outside the group; it identifies global changes such as, "Well, this is what is happening in Europe."
- They can connect it all to the future vision.
- They can apply their analytical critiquing skills to identifying mistakes made in the past; for example, "See, we overlooked this in the eighties, and that's why this problem developed."

Looking at the past provides *NT*s with a systematic understanding and principles to guide planning for the future.

Acknowledging the Losses in Change

Recognizing the past provides an entree into another important issue during times of change. When people look back over the history of their group, each person remembers people who have left, projects that are over, systems that no longer exist, ideas that got lost, environments that supported their work—the "good old days." It's important to acknowledge the losses, and not to ignore the past. In order to let go of the past, some way of grieving may need to be provided.1

STs and NTs may attempt to minimize their own and others' losses, especially when emotions are involved. They tend to assess their emotions with logic, as if asking themselves, "Does it make sense to feel this way?" If it doesn't, they will usually try to ignore or suppress the emotions. They compartmentalize or bury them, keeping their feelings separate from their actions and not expressing them. Sometimes that works, and it doesn't feel like much of a loss. Other times, long-term regrets can result from the failure to acknowledge the loss and grieve.

SFs and NFs can usually identify a number of losses and the emotions connected to each. Yet many organizations ignore the fact that changes involve loss, which makes processing the emotions connected with loss more difficult. A lot of Fs get stuck in being angry because their losses are not acknowledged and support is not given for grieving. They want and need to talk about loss in order to move into the future. Recognizing the past, valuing its lessons, and grieving its passing are important benefits of this step.

The final step in recognizing the past is in bringing forward the perspectives and knowledge gained to use them in dealing with the present situation and future challenges. An important question people ask is, "What is in this historical perspective for me in dealing with the present and future?" People of different types have indicated the following questions as helpful to them in bringing this information forward.

Sensing and Thinking (ST)	Sensing and Feeling (SF)	Intuition and Feeling (NF)	Intuition and Thinking (NT)
• When, in the past, did I deal successfully with a change? What did I do that was helpful then? • What can I bring forward from that experience that will apply to the current situation?	• When in the past did I deal successfully with a change? • Who and what helped me to do that? • Where did I find support in the past? • How did I deal with my emotions? • What can I bring forward from my experience that will help me deal successfully with the present situation?	• What is at the heart of this group? • What is this group's identity? • How has the group dealt with change in the past? • What would help this group right now? • How can we move toward the future?	• How does this present situation compare to past crises/change situations? • What is the context, the overall explanatory pattern that provides perspective on the current situation? • What mistakes did we make with past changes? • What can we do to avoid making those same mistakes?

Given the current changes in your work, what is important to you about the past? What successes and experiences have you had? What's hard to let go of? After acknowledging the past and being able to grieve, people are better equipped to focus on change.

3. Decide Specifically What Needs to Be Changed

The questions to explore here are: What are we doing now that we want to continue doing? and What do we need to do differently?

Type influences how people approach the question, What needs to be changed? We have found the following combinations of preferences particularly important.

Introversion and Sensing (ISTJ, ISFJ, ISTP, ISFP): "What shall we change?"	Introversion and Intuition (INFJ, INTJ, INFP, INTP): What shall we change?"
• "As little as possible." • Want continuity in their work lives • Accept changes that will clearly produce better results • Want to change incrementally, in a step-by-step process, evaluating each step before moving on to make more changes	• "Let me think about it." • The intangibles—the vision or the direction—may need to be changed first. • It has to fit with the internal vision, value, or principle. • See change in global and long-range context—want the present to lead to that
Their primary motivation to change: **It's the responsible thing to do.**	Their primary motivation for change: **a match with the vision, value, or principle.**

Extraversion and Sensing (ESTP, ESFP, ESTJ, ESFJ):	**Extraversion and Intuition (ENFP, ENTP, ENFJ, ENTJ):**
"What shall we change?"	"What shall we change?"
• "Make only the practical, necessary changes." Change only things that aren't working properly. • If it's in bad shape, change a lot; if it's not too bad, change a little. • Focus on the results to assess whether we need to change: "If it ain't broke, don't fix it." • "If it's broke, fix it now!"	• "As much as possible!" • As fast as possible—a lot of changes at the same time • As far-reaching as possible—to encompass everything • Failure is no big deal; just try something else.
Their primary motivation for change: **what's not working.**	Their primary motivation for change: **an interesting new idea.**

As you approach the current changes, what will you need to change in your day-to-day work? Can you make those changes happen? Who else needs to be involved? Once you understand how to look at change, it's time to look at individual roles and responsibilities.

4. Getting What You Need

Organizations are so focused on the desired future and so busy trying to find a way to make it work that they may not take time to pay attention to the needs of the people. We think this is shortsighted, but our focus here is how you can take responsibility for getting your own needs met, regardless of whether your organization is sensitive to them.

People have very different needs during change. The first step is to identify clearly what your needs are.[2] For example, the following has been identified:

Extraverts need involvement in the process, opportunity to talk about the changes with other people, and an active role in implementing the change. **Introverts** need time and space to reflect on the changes, to fit them into their internal picture or system, and an opportunity to contribute the result of their reflections.

Judging types need things to be clear and on a timetable. The end needs to be achievable and in sight—they want to be able to look ahead to when this will be done. **Perceiving** types need flexibility, space to try things out, to let things emerge, and to reopen things that need to be revisited.

As you consider your type, do the needs that are listed fit for you? What other things would be helpful? Is there a way to get those resources and information? Again, paying attention to personality may make your changes go more smoothly.

What Each Type Needs During Times of Change[3]

ISTJs need to	ISFJs need to	INFJs need to	INTJs need to
• gather specific, realistic reasons for the changes • find lots of practical data to support the reasons • take leadership in setting goals and creating timelines, plans and structures • use their experiences to give substance to the vision	• gather realistic data about why they have to change • take time to adjust and plan calmly, at their own pace • see a well-thought-out plan that recognizes the personal impacts of the changes • receive understanding and support for dealing with their losses	• see the biggest possible picture of the change, of the future • be included in conceptualizing and deciding on the changes • take some time and space to reflect and process it on their own • feel supported and have opportunities to support others	• see the global picture • have independence, time and space—the opportunity to figure things out for themselves on their own • be in on the planning • to have action, and closure

ISTPs need to	ISFPs need to	INFPs need to	INTPs need to
• have freedom • take action • evaluate what's working and what isn't • plan and troubleshoot as they go	• receive respect for their attachments, including their space • get information about what is going on • feel support for themselves and the opportunity to support others • take time to adjust and to process on their own	• be independent, come to their own conclusions—not be pushed • feel that others respect their values • take time to collect and process information • be accepted for who they are	• be independent, to apply their own analyses and standards to the situation • see the big picture and affect the planning • gather a great deal of information at their own pace • act in open-ended time frames and not be pushed

ESTPs need to	ESFPs need to	ENFPs need to	ENTPs need to
• take action and keep moving • be independent • talk with like-minded people • make on-the-spot decisions and use their resourcefulness	• be involved and get others involved • get moving • enjoy the process and add their enthusiasm and humor • talk about their observations and feelings	• be included in the process • pay attention to the impacts on people and support them • verbalize the positive possibilities along with the losses • gather a lot of information from others and talk about it	• act independently • talk about their ideas for the change • generate further possibilities with enthusiasm • find a way to buy in and play a leadership role
ESTJs need to	**ESFJs need to**	**ENFJs need to**	**ENTJs need to**
• see the rationale and the data behind it • plan what needs to be done to implement • have access to necessary resources • take charge and just do it	• receive lots of support and have time to support others • get lots of information and talk about it • help people feel good about the changes • be appreciated for who they are and what they contribute to others	• receive lots of positive feedback and support • have their insights and values listened to and validated • have time to support others and be appreciated for playing that role • be reassured about continuing relationships and others' counting on them	• play a leadership role in moving the change forward • have their analysis and solutions respected • be allowed to command resources—technology and people • see positive possibilities in the future

Example Revisited

Let's revisit the opening scenario to see how a type perspective can help us understand what was going on inside each individual, the inner dialogue. Remember that our characters are:

Leader, ENTP

Executive council, ENTJs and INTJs

Tony, ISTJ

Nancy, ENFP

Linda, INTP

Jean, ESTJ

Paul, ESFJ

Leader (ENTP): "We are announcing a new initiative, XYZ. The executive council has studied various options and decided this is the way Warren Products needs to go.

"Here are the plan, the schedule, and the training sessions to teach everyone to work in this new system. It's going to take a great deal of work and commitment from everyone.

"I'm excited about the plan: It gives us an opportunity to position ourselves to meet the challenges of the future. I know you'll all get on board and make this work."

Leader's (and the executive council's) inner dialogue: We've got to shake things up and get this company moving or we're going to be left behind. This is the cutting edge, the latest thinking in what companies need to do—the Harvard Business Review had an exciting article on this.

I'm not sure we can get our current people to move along fast enough. Some of them are so resistant—anything we suggest, they complain and whine.

If we really paint the picture of the future with enthusiasm, surely they'll see that this is the answer and get on board.

We've just got to slam-dunk this change. They can get on board or find another train.

A group of employees who work together as a team goes to lunch after the meeting and discusses the leader's presentation:

Jean (ESTJ): "Another one of these stupid changes. Can you believe it? Remember when they announced the restructuring a year ago? It just hasn't worked. We couldn't even figure out how to route our mail for the first three months. People still don't know who to call. And we sure haven't seen all the savings they promised."

Jean's inner dialogue: I could support this change if they answer these questions: What's the point: How will the result be different from what we have now and why is that desirable? What was wrong that needed to be fixed? Have they thought about when they have tried similar things in the past, what worked and didn't, why they are trying it now? What procedures are in place to support us during the change? How will the change make our daily work better? And I want to be asked for input and have my suggestions utilized or explain why my suggestions won't work. I want the opportunity to critique the plans and the process, to influence midcourse corrections.

Paul (ESFJ): "XYZ is going to be so hard on everyone. People are going to be so upset. Is this going to affect our salaries? I can feel my stomach tightening up already."

Paul's inner dialogue: I'm really worried about Tony; he gets so stressed about this stuff. And Jean gets so cranky. I wish she would be more positive. Nancy's going to be bringing in books for all of us to read and giving us all these new ideas—I hope I can understand them. I wonder what my boss thinks about this. I bet she's really behind it, and I need to support her. I hope it doesn't mean our team will have to

break up. Linda's really checked out—I hope she doesn't pull away from all of us. I wonder what Terry thinks about this—I need to talk with him. And with Margaret—she's on the inside and really understands the leader's thinking.

Nancy (ENFP): "Well, now wait a minute. Just because restructuring didn't work well, doesn't mean this can't. I can see some real exciting possibilities here."

Nancy's inner dialogue: You know, this reminds me of what Jack was talking about at our networking meeting last month. It seemed exciting—I think we're on to something. I need to call Jack to get some more information from him. Oh, and Diane too—I think she said her company did something like this. I think I can help Tony see how this could work. I wish Jean wouldn't be so negative and critical about everything. I hope this doesn't mean that they're going to lay anyone off. How are they going to help people do this? Have they thought about that? I told them two years ago they ought to go to something like this—now they act like it's a brand-new idea they've thought of.

Tony (ISTJ): "I'm feeling really confused. What exactly are we supposed to do? What's going to happen to our department? How are we going to meet our customers' needs and keep our regular work going? This will be so much work! We've already got too much to do."

Tony's inner dialogue: What data did they have that led them to make this decision? I spent a lot of time developing the procedures that make my department run smoothly. I don't see any point in letting those go. I'm worried about the people I'm responsible for—how will they get their work done? How will I get my work done? Who's tried this kind of change before—what was their experience? Is our situation the same? Will it work here? I'm afraid I don't have the knowledge base, the experience, to do what this change will require of me. Where will I get it?

Jean: *"I agree."*

Paul: *"Oh, Tony, you know your job. I know you're worried about keeping up with all your work, but you're so good at what you do, you'll be able to handle it. We know we can always count on you."*

Nancy: *"That's right. We're a really competent group of people here. We can handle this. Give it a chance."*

Jean: *"Yes, **we're** competent, but I'm not sure **they** are."*

Tony: *"And I don't have time to do all this new stuff! They're going to throw out some 'great' ideas and then leave it to us to figure out how to do them, as usual. It's just too much."*

Paul: *"Linda, you're very quiet. What do you think about this?"*

Linda (INTP): *"Look, I don't think we can tell anything at this point. Let's not get too excited or worried about it. They will probably change their mind again next week, and it won't ever even happen. We can worry about what we need to do when we actually see something happening."*

Linda's inner dialogue: This is just the change-of-the-month. They sure didn't give us much information about their rationale—they're just scrambling for something, anything, to cover their mismanagement. According to what I've read, a lot of companies have had real problems putting in the kind of system they're thinking of. I wonder if they really researched this change. I don't know why people have to get so emotional about these things. These things happen. You just have to roll with the punches. If they'll just leave me alone and let me do my work, I'll be okay.

Jean: *"Mark my words: There are going to be problems, no matter what happens!"*

Moving Our Group Forward

The next morning at a team meeting, the group had not moved much beyond their initial reactions to the announcement, and these seemed to be getting in the way of their work on an important task. Suddenly, Nancy reminded the group that they had found the MBTI very helpful in understanding their team interactions and how to deal more effectively with each other. She made a suggestion: "Maybe we could use that for a few minutes to see if it can help us understand our reactions—what's going on and what we need to do about it."

The group entered into an animated discussion of their type-related needs in relationship to information, communication, and decision-making. This discussion produced a lot of energy, some fun and humor, and, eventually, some clarity about what different members of the group needed to be able to understand and to participate in the XYZ initiative. They made the following commitments:

Jean (ESTJ) committed to:

- getting information about the reasons for deciding on the XYZ initiative;
- getting her questions answered—what was wrong, how will this be better;
- seeing how she can offer her critiques in a useful way.

Once she gets the information she needs, she'll be ready to act.

Tony (ISTJ) is committed to:

- gathering a lot more practical data about what was behind the decision;

- identifying what actual steps and specifics are involved in implementing XYZ.

Tony is overloaded with work, yet he said, "This will be interesting to me. I can make time."

Paul (ESFJ) committed to:

- finding out the executive council's plans for taking care of people during this time of change;
- identifying how he could personally be involved in their plans.

If those plans did not seem sufficient, he would offer to head up a task force to develop needed support plans.

Nancy (ENFP) committed to:

- finding other people who want to get together at breakfast meetings to explore the possibilities she sees;
- calling her networking contacts to gather more information and share that with others in the organization.

And she said to Paul, "Let me know what you find out about how they're going to respond to people and the people issues—that has to happen and I'll support your group if the executive council isn't paying attention to the people side."

Linda (INTP) committed to:

- researching the problems that others had found in implementing XYZ;

- summarizing those problems briefly (with references to further information);
- suggesting ways Warren can anticipate and avoid such problems.

She will write this up for the executive committee, and offer to continue researching in order to find the latest ideas and information on XYZ, the potential problems, and ways they can be anticipated.

Dealing More Effectively with Organizational Change

Usually, employees first hear about a change through an announcement: Here's what the company is going to do. For the employees, this change is **imposed,** and initial doubts or resistance are natural reactions toward the people imposing the changes.

The fundamental requirement for dealing effectively with changes is to find a way to participate, make a meaningful contribution, and become a part of the change effort: to make an **intentional** change. If the organization does not include employees in the decision-making process, how can people take ownership?

By yourself or with others you trust, look at the following questions to identify what you need to become an active participant, rather than a passive (and complaining) victim:

PARTICIPATING IN THE CHANGE PROCESS

1. How does your past experience help you in this situation?
   - What can you bring forward to contribute in this situation?
2. Use your type to analyze why you are feeling/thinking the way you are about the changes.
   - Does the decision seem to ignore your need for a logical rationale?
   - Does it seem to ignore the impact on people?
   - What's missing for you?
3. Use your type to see what kinds of information you need to seek out.
   - Practical data?
   - The big picture of the future?
   - What's wrong with the way things are now?
   - Possibilities for you?
4. How does the time frame of the change work for your type?
   - Too open?
   - Too tight?
   - Can you see ways to adjust the schedule and structure?
5. For what reasons do you like to be included?
   - Your ideas?
   - Your experience?
   - Your critiques?
   - Your support?
6. Remember, type knowledge can help you identify your own needs and what will help you to be at your best. Then you need to be responsible for yourself—to find the ways to meet those needs that have been identified.

CHAPTER 9

STRESS

ver find yourself saying these things?

"This job is driving me crazy!"
"If only the boss would get off my back, I could get something done!"
"If only the phone would stop ringing!"
"One more last-minute rush job and I'm out of here!"

The kinds of things we've been talking about in this book are all potential stressors at work:

- miscommunications
- not enough time, too much to do
- too many meetings (or not enough meetings)
- the scope, constancy, and fast pace of change
- personality conflicts with colleagues
- difficult bosses
- teams that don't work well together

The workplace today is stressful. However, what stresses one person may not always stress others: One's personal experiences with stress may be type related.

Interaction of Type Preferences and Stress

The following are some examples of things that particularly stress people with different preferences.

Extraversion—Introversion

- Being left alone to complete a project
  (Stresses E, Energizes I)
- Interruptions that distract from focus and concentration
  (Stresses I, Energize E)

*Eric (**Extraverted** preference) and Isabella (**Introverted** preference) are working together on a project. Phase I calls on them to talk to people all over the company. You know how that is: leave a message, get a call back at their convenience, and so on. Eric finds himself highly energized by the ongoing interruptions. Isabella goes home every night drained and irritable.*

Phase II of the project means each needs to compile the data from all those calls. Eric finds he has to come out of his office frequently—working alone is deadly for his energy. Isabella, on the other hand, is feeling great!

Sensing—Intuition

- Brainstorming
  (Stresses S, Energize N)

- Collection of specific data for a project
    (Stresses N, Energize S)

*Samuel (**Sensing** preference) and Natalie (**Intuitive** preference) are attending a team-building session. The day's first assignment—brainstorming in order to come up with as many definitions as possible for "team"—leaves Samuel feeling uninterested and wondering how relevant brainstorming even is and Natalie feeling really energized. Later when the team looks at its year-end financial report, Samuel is really interested and Natalie is bored, bored, bored!*

Thinking—Feeling

- Making personal connections with colleagues
    (Stresses T, Energizes F)
- Critiquing an idea or project, finding the flaws
    (Stresses F, Energizes T)

*Terri (**Thinking** preference) supervises Fred (**Feeling** preference) and finds his need to talk about his friends and family and ask her about her weekends to be idle chitchat. Fred finds that the talk helps him feel connected to Terri in a real way. When Terri asks Fred to save it for lunchtime, Fred feels like a gap has appeared in their relationship. When Terri asks him to critique what's wrong with her project proposal, Fred worries a lot about it; he feels like it could be painful for both of them.*

Judging—Perceiving

- When an important project is thrown off schedule
    (Stresses J, Energizes P)

- A tightly structured project with firm timelines
  (Stresses P, Energizes J)

*Julie (**Judging** preference) and Patti (**Perceiving** preference) have the responsibility for getting monthly reports out to the field in a timely fashion. Julie really likes the firm timelines they've worked out to make this happen. Patti feels really hemmed in—until a last-minute breakdown in the copy machine throws Julie into high stress and energizes Patti to find another quickly. What a great feeling to pull it off!*

Typical Work Activities and Type Preferences

As you can see, having to work in a way that goes against your natural style can cause stress. Being able to find some balance can help alleviate the stress. So when Isabella (I) had to do the phone work that drained her, she found that Introverted time compiling the reports brought her energy back up. Sometimes in our work we can vary our routines to include the kind of time or space we need. Think about your job and the tasks you do. Can you find any way to work out a more balanced approach for your own needs?

To help you look at your job according to type, you might wish to consider the following lists of common activities that take place at work by the different type preferences most associated with those activities. Check what your job calls for and compare those activities with your type preferences. A mismatch can be a cause of stress in your life.

Extraverted Activities
- working together with others
- talking on the phone a lot

- interacting with others frequently
- acting quickly
- having variety

- getting frequent verbal feedback

Introverted Activities
- working alone
- using E-mail to communicate
- uninterrupted time to concentrate
- reflecting before acting
- being able to focus in depth on one thing
- getting careful, considered, private feedback

Sensing Activities
- paying attention to realities
- using proven ways to do things
- attending to detail
- making sure the facts are accurate
- drawing on experience
- being practical

Intuitive Activities
- paying attention to insights
- seeking new ways to do old things
- wanting an overview
- making sure the meaning of the facts is obvious
- drawing on possibilities
- being complex

Thinking Activities
- analyzing situations objectively
- setting criteria and standards
- critiquing and spotting flaws

- focusing on tasks
- using logic to make decisions

- asking questions to clarify ideas

Feeling Activities
- assessing situations by personal experience
- adjusting to individual differences and needs
- noticing and appreciating what is positive
- focusing on process and people
- using empathy and personal values to make decisions
- seeing questions as emphasizing differences, not creating harmony

Judging Activities

- organizing themselves and others
- counting on planning to pull it off
- needing time frames and deadlines
- setting things up to avoid last-minute rushes

- finishing off and moving on
- developing contingency plans

Perceiving Activities

- allowing the structure to emerge from the process
- counting on inner timing to pull it off
- needing flexibility about time frames and deadlines
- setting things up to take advantage of last-minute energy
- keeping open for reevaluation
- hoping for surprises

Most jobs require you to do a variety of activities, including things on all these preference lists. However, if you spend most of your time performing nonpreferred activities, this can lead to work-related stress. Looking back at the list, which of the "out-of-type" activities in your work life, if any, cause you the most stress?

What Can You Do?

1. Can you trade some of these activities with someone else who does not find them stressful?
   - "If you'll give the report, I'll write it" (said the Introvert to the Extravert).
   - "If you'll figure out the budget categories, I'll fill in the details" (said the Sensor to the Intuitive).
2. Are there ways you can intersperse those activities with ones more congenial to you?
   - Most of us can do "out-of-type" activities for a while, as long as we have frequent breaks.
   - Reward yourself. If I finish the report this morning,

I'll ask Bob to go to lunch with me. (A reward for the Extravert.)

3. Can you reframe or recast an activity to include things more congenial to you?
   - As a Feeling type, when I'm asked to critique someone's plan, can I see this as an opportunity also to give them support and coaching?

4. Do you need to look for a different type of work or for different roles within your current job situation?
   - Can you rotate into another position?
   - Can you switch roles, from the front lines to behind the scenes? Or vice versa?

Of course there are many other things that cause stress beyond your type preferences in the workplace. Sorry! We can't help with those in this book!

Some Warning Signs of Stress: Type Exaggeration

You may already have some ways to recognize when you are experiencing stress. A type perspective can identify some others that you may not be aware of. These can be helpful not only in recognizing your own stress, but also in recognizing signs of stress in others.

Even with all our best efforts to minimize stress, there are still times and situations that are out of our control: a deadline that requires us to work long, long hours; changes in the workplace that cause us to have to change all our routines; being overwhelmed with the amount of work and the responsibilities we have, with more piled on all the time. In such times, everyone can lose perspective, can be distracted, can lose focus, and can feel pulled in a hundred different directions. It's hard to work effectively at such times.

As we explained in Chapter 7, each type has a driving force, which is called the dominant function. It's usually the part that you lead with, use the most, and that you find most comfortable. During a time of stress, it is natural that people try to "get on top of things" by using their favorite, most reliable process almost exclusively. The problem is, this can cause us to become out of balance, lead to an exaggeration of this favorite process, and to the ignoring of the other parts of the personality that normally provide the balance needed.

What Does Exaggeration Look Like in Different Types?

The following graphics give specifics each type has reported about their exaggerated behaviors. Then we give an example of how this looks when leading a meeting.

EXTRAVERTS

Normal, Balanced	Somewhat Exaggerated	Out of Control
S	S	S
scanning immediate environment	focused on one aspect of immediate environment	obsessed with that one aspect
experiencing the moment	excessive focus on enjoyment of the moment	overindulgence in physical pleasure—This is the only moment!

Exaggerated Extraverted Sensing (ESTP and ESFP)

Sally, an ESTP, was under great pressure at work. Her department was faced with new government regulations that would seriously affect the way they worked, and her superiors were putting pressure on her to deal with them quickly. She started her meeting by saying, "We all need to understand the current challenges facing us because of the new government regulations. Let me show you some data that will make the challenges clear." Sally then started to go through twenty-five chart pages she had carefully prepared, each showing the data in a slightly different way. Members of the group began interrupting, saying they understood the challenge and had ideas for solutions, but Sally could not let go of her charts—she felt that everyone had to understand the data fully, completely, and in detail before they would understand as well as she did and be ready to move on to suggesting solutions.

Normal, Balanced	Somewhat Exaggerated	Out of Control
N	N	N
see the possibilities	scattered among all the possibilities	totally distracted, swamped by possibilities
enthusiastic	Involve everyone *now*!	manic

Exaggerated Extraverted Intuition (ENFP and ENTP)

Sue's (ENFP) style in leading meetings was usually warm and enthusiastic, and normally her group responded by supporting her exciting new ideas. In this meeting, however, the group did not respond positively and become involved in their usual manner. She worked to get everyone more excited and involved, but the group seemed bored and had low energy. Sue began to shift from enthusiastic to performing, almost putting on a show. She began telling wild, unrelated, and shocking stories to the group, trying to get their attention and a reaction.

Normal, Balanced	Somewhat Exaggerated	Out of Control
T	T	T
logical	officious about their logic	coldly dissecting, analytical—Mr. Spock personified
organized	controlled, controlling— We will be organized!	rigid—The *only* way to be organized is *my* way!

Exaggerated Extraverted Thinking (ESTJ and ENTJ)

Jack, an ESTJ, began his meeting by presenting an organized, structured agenda based on the suggestions of the group from the previous week's meeting. However, several new situations had arisen in the last week, and group members suggested that the agenda needed some modification. Jack felt that the group needed to make several decisions from the original agenda so that his own work could progress. He began to glare at people who raised new issues and insisted on going back to the posted agenda. The group resented this and began confronting him. He would not budge in the order or the topics covered and became more and more rigid, interrupting people who were off topic to get them back on (his) task.

Normal, Balanced	Somewhat Exaggerated	Out of Control
F	F	F
caring for others	knowing what's best for others	self-righteous about knowing and impose that on others

| responsive to people's needs | intrusive probing for your needs | telling others what they need and forcing it on them |

Exaggerated Extraverted Feeling (ESFJ and ENFJ)

Jackie, an ENFJ, felt very insecure in her new job. She had never had supervisory responsibility before and was not sure she had the skills and experience necessary to manage her department. She was particularly worried about two employees who always seemed to have different perspectives and to take pleasure in disagreeing with each other. She was determined to start off right by finding ways to get them to work together better. At her first meeting, an important disagreement arose between the two and Julie immediately said, "Now, I'm sure we can find a middle ground here and come to agreement." When the two rejected this approach and escalated their argument, she again broke in and said, "Now, Bill, you don't really mean that. I know that deep down inside you respect Jack's position and experience. Jack, I know you really like Bill, but you just don't know how to show it. I want the two of you to shake hands and then go to lunch together—talk about yourselves and your families, tell each other something important about yourself, really open up and share who you are. After that I bet you'll be able to work together just fine."

INTROVERTS

Normal, Balanced	*Somewhat Exaggerated*	*Out of Control*
S	S	S
select the "right" details	see **only** the "right" details	obsessed, fixated on THE ONLY IMPORTANT DETAIL

| realistic | certain about what is real here | dogmatic about their reality |

Exaggerated Introverted Sensing (ISTJ and ISFJ)

Sandy's ISTJ style of leading a meeting was straightforward and realistic. She carefully planned and prepared what she was going to say ahead of time so that all the pieces were in place and in the correct order. After all, having the correct data in order was crucial for her in making good decisions, and she was sure it was the right way for everyone else. Sandy began the meeting as she had planned. Group members began asking questions that she thought were unrelated to the present topic but were on her agenda for later. She said, "We'll deal with that in thirty minutes or so; we need to do this first." As the group increasingly resisted her careful structure, Sandy more firmly insisted on taking the topics in order, feeling that the solid structure of information had to be there. When the group became unruly and began making wisecracks, she tuned out the room and the group, continuing with her planned presentations.

Normal, Balanced	Somewhat Exaggerated	Out of Control
N	**N**	**N**
see connections	complexify the connections	The GRAND UNIFYING THEORY OF THE UNIVERSE—Everything is connected to everything
clarity of vision	surety about their vision	arrogance about the correctness of their vision

Exaggerated Introverted Intuition (INFJ and INTJ)

Pat, an INFJ, read an exciting new book that led him to form a vision of transforming management in his organization. He called a meeting of the managers to present his vision. Several managers indicated that they felt the current structure was working fine and others raised questions about the specifics of this vision. Both of those issues seemed beside the point to Pat—the point was his exciting new vision. Pat became irritated, but didn't show it. Then he began shutting off questions, saying there was no need for further discussion, this was the way it was going to be. No one could make any headway and no one fully understood him. They could not figure out what he was saying or what they were supposed to do.

Normal, Balanced	*Somewhat Exaggerated*	*Out of Control*
T	**T**	**T**
search for truths and explanations	focus on finding *the* truth	obsessive insistence on *the truth* I have found
critique in an analytical way	internal critical monologues (diatribes): No one knows. . . . They're all stupid. . . .	arrogant dismissal of all other perspectives and people

Exaggerated Introverted Thinking (ISTP and INTP)

Al, an INTP, went into his meeting with a clear sense of the decisions that needed to be made by the group. The group had a number of other items that were important to them and began discussing them. Al felt comfortable with a certain amount of off-the-topic discussion until he got worried that there would not be enough time for his issues. His upset continued when some members of the group had a different perspective than his on the issues he had already carefully thought through and figured out the correct course of action. He was sure he was right, yet they wanted to discuss those issues at great lengths. Al then began pontificating, explaining the logic of his positions, insisting on his perspective and analysis, bitingly critiquing the issues raised by others, and sarcastically rejecting their concerns.

Normal, Balanced	*Somewhat Exaggerated*	*Out of Control*
F	**F**	**F**
idealistic	righteous idealism— My ideal is the "right"ideal	demagogic— You *will* believe this
loyal	defensively loyal	embattled martyrs

Exaggerated Introverted Feeling (ISFP and INFP)

Ron, an ISFP, headed up a committee to organize an international conference. He planned "the greatest conference ever"—he could "see" it. He put incredible time and energy into planning every aspect, even the most minute ones. A few months before the conference, the organization's president attended a committee meeting to check on the planning and give advice. At one point, he raised questions about the high cost of the "wonderful keynote speaker."

Ron was wounded and thought, Why couldn't people understand how important this keynote speaker was? She would set the tone for the entire experience. Ron had worked so hard to make this conference special, to secure the services of this famous speaker: How could people criticize him and be so unappreciative of all he had done?

Getting Back in Balance

In all these cases, the individuals were under stress and tried to deal with it by using their favorite functions. In an attempt to deal with the stress, they overused this favorite function, stopped using other normal parts of their personalities, and got out of balance. Their normal way of dealing with problems became exaggerated.

This exaggeration seldom works to get a situation back under control. These individuals have lost their normal repertoire of adaptable responses. They have become rigid caricatures of their normal selves, with little flexibility available to them.

Others are negatively impacted by people in an exaggerated state. In dealing with such people, you may sometimes find yourself clamming up and silently resisting. At other times, you may push back, arguing with the sweeping statements or the intensity of their expression. You may feel embarrassed because the person seems out of control, and you may even wish you could just leave.

Because people in an exaggerated state are out of balance, the most helpful way of dealing with this—whether it is you or someone else—is a break, a time-out to restore some perspective and balance. If you recognize that you are in a stress-related state of exaggeration, request a break and a later return to the topic. You could say something like: "I'd like to have a chance to reflect on this more. Can we go on to some other items on our agenda and return to this later?" or "Could we take a five-minute break?"

When you recognize that someone else is becoming dogmatic and exaggerated, once again, a break or some space is usually helpful. Try saying, "Wait a minute. Let's sit down for a minute and take a look at it," or "This is a really important topic, and I'm having a little trouble focusing on it right now.

Could we take a five-minute break and then take another look at it?"

Normally, some type of break or time-out will restore the balance and help people get back on track to deal more effectively with the problems and stresses.

Extreme Stress:
The "Grip" of the Inferior Function

What about when there's no time for a break, the pressure mounts, you're tired or sick, and the stress just keeps on building? When stress becomes too extreme, what happens is a total imbalance in the personality and, in this situation, the parts of yourself that you use least often can suddenly erupt and be expressed in ways that are shocking and upsetting to you and to those around you. These eruptions are not just exaggerations of your normal personality, but instead are expressions of parts of yourself that neither you nor others are used to seeing. They seem totally out of character. People say things such as "I don't know what came over me," or "I just wasn't myself." For more information on this process, you may wish to read Naomi Quenk's book *Beside Ourselves*, which describes the grip of the inferior function in great detail.[1]

Though many personal elements enter into these eruptions, the theory of psychological type gives pointers to characteristic forms they may take for particular types. For example, those who prefer Extraversion are typically pushed inside themselves, and may become locked inside and unable to use their normal verbal abilities, while those who prefer Introversion may uncharacteristically "explode," expressing Extraverted parts of themselves.

All personality types experience these eruptions as upsetting and usually embarrassing. This is because we are not usually competent in these unused areas. Our behavior is childish and our perspective is either/or, with no middle ground.

We can revisit our meetings where people were in an exaggerated state to understand what can happen next, if the balance is not restored.

The Extraverts

EXTRAVERTED SENSING (ESTP AND ESFP): SALLY AND HER CHARTS

When more people begin to lose interest in Sally's charts and ask her to move on, she will be pushed inside, where her thoughts swirl around. Suddenly she "knows" that her department and the organization will not survive this challenge, that people do not and cannot understand, that she will be out of a job and unable to find another because of her failure here. As the inner picture and feelings become overwhelmingly clear to her, Sally becomes cranky with the group: "I can see that none of you are interested in this. You obviously don't understand the seriousness of the problem. I'm calling a halt to this meeting." She then abruptly leaves.

Sally's least-used and least-developed aspect is Introverted Intuition. Her "knowing" was most likely not accurate because she hadn't developed much of her Intuition, but to her in this moment, her Intuition was her reality. The only possibility she saw was negative.

EXTRAVERTED INTUITION (ENFP AND ENTP): SUE AND HER EXCITING IDEAS

When the group doesn't respond positively to her ideas, Sue gets pushed inside, becoming quiet, directing her energy and attention away from her exciting ideas toward specific "Sensing" details in the environment: The room was not arranged properly, the lunch (delicious, in reality) was wrong, the markers didn't work right. Others saw this as a "picky" focus on what were to them unimportant details, inaccurately perceived.

Sue's least-used and -developed part is Introverted Sensing. Focusing on specific environmental details is deenergizing for her, not productive for the group, and unsettling to everyone. Unimportant details became the main focus for her.

EXTRAVERTED THINKING (ENTJ AND ESTJ): JACK AND HIS STRUCTURED AGENDA

Jack gets pushed inside when group members make suggestions for changing the meeting format, and he experiences a confused morass of horrible feelings. He is convinced that he is a failure as a leader and obviously not competent. Nothing he's done has gone right, the group doesn't respect him, and, in fact, they shouldn't—he's "no good." The group sees him becoming emotional, sensitive to criticism, and taking everything they say personally. He seems emotionally out of control, being judgmental, angry, attacking.

Jack's least-used and least-developed aspect is Introverted Feeling. This sinking into undeveloped Introverted Feeling is upsetting to Jack, the group does not know how to deal with this suddenly irrational person, and, later, Jack is very embarrassed when he remembers his uncharacteristically emotional behavior. Childish reactions and erroneous values took over his usual logical thinking.

EXTRAVERTED FEELING (ESFJ AND ENFJ): JACKIE'S ATTEMPTS TO HELP

When Bob and Jack resist her suggestions about how they can get along, our new supervisor, Jackie, is pushed inside, where she first begins directing hypercritical remarks toward herself: "See, I knew I couldn't do this. I'll never succeed; it's just like everything else I try to do—I'm a total failure." Then, typically, she lashes out at others, accusing them of deliberately trying to sabotage the group. She uses her sensitive understanding of other people to focus in on their individual weaknesses, exposing them in front of the group.

Jackie's least-used and -developed part is Introverted Thinking. When she gets caught in this, she becomes illogical and uses biting, unreasonable criticism instead of the good aspects of Thinking. The group is astonished by this nice-to-nasty twist, and later Jackie is horrified to remember her unkind, critical attacks.

In all these cases of Extraverts, the move into the uncharacteristic part of themselves removes their energy from their external activities and they turn inward, thus appearing to others to be distant, cold, or depressed.

The Introverts

Remember that Introverts get pushed into their less comfortable Extraverted parts.

INTROVERTED SENSING (ISTJ AND ISFJ): SANDY'S CAREFULLY PREPARED STAFF MEETING

The staff meeting has fallen apart, and Sandy's carefully structured meeting is in shambles. She suddenly draws herself up and erupts at the group: "Do you realize what will happen if we don't take care of these issues? I've worked hard to put this together and you just sit there making jokes. You're all going to fall on your face, and I won't pick up after you this time." The group, naturally, is taken aback by this sudden explosion from the normally calm Sandy. They feel guilty about their behavior, but also angry about Sandy's intense and unfair judgments.

Sandy's least-used and -developed aspect is Extraverted Intuition. When she gets pushed into this, she makes sweeping statements about the future, which are almost always negative and fraught with disaster.

INTROVERTED INTUITION (INFJ AND INTJ):
PAT'S INSIGHTS AND VISION

When it became clear that the group was not understanding and enthusiastically accepting his vision, Pat abruptly shifted his focus to attack people in the meeting angrily: "Oh sure, the present system works great. That's why you, Liz, lost three of your best people last year. David, that's why you overspent your budget by twenty-three-and-a-half percent. Phyllis, what are your training expenditures to date? What percent of the budget have you spent?"

Pat's least-used and least-developed part is Extraverted Sensing. When he gets into this, he focuses on details that are normally unimportant to him and really irrelevant to the discussion. No one was anticipating needing to know those details, and his inquiries felt very unfair to them.

INTROVERTED THINKING (ISTP AND INTP):
AL'S IMPORTANT DECISIONS

As the meeting degenerated and most of the group shut up, Mary continued to challenge Al's ideas. Al finally exploded, slamming his hand on the table and yelling at Mary: "You can just leave this meeting, right now. Get out!"

Al's least-used and least-developed part is Extraverted Feeling. Like most other Introverted Thinking types, Al's Extraverted Feeling was not developed; instead, it took the form of exaggerated and inappropriate expression of uncontrolled emotions. His eruption was personal, illogical, unreasonable, and unfair—a distorted expression of Al's least-developed part.

INTROVERTED FEELING (ISFP AND INFP):
RON'S WONDERFUL CONFERENCE

The president, not understanding what was going on inside Ron, suggested some less expensive alternatives for the keynote program. Ron finally exploded: "You don't understand the people in this organization. You're such a bureaucrat—you can't see beyond the numbers to what's really the heart and soul of this organization and our mission. I can't continue with this lack of trust. I resign!"

Ron's least-used and -developed part was Extraverted Thinking. When he erupted into this, his Thinking came out as an attack, rather than a balanced critique, as Thinkers typically do.

In all these Introverted cases, the move of energy is into Extraverted expressions.

A Recap: Important Points
About Using Type in Stress Management

Helping Yourself

The temptation is to forget these experiences as soon as possible, to say, "I wasn't myself," and try not to think of them.

However, we suggest a different approach. Should you find yourself in the grip of such an experience:

1. Pay attention—you really need a break. Go for a walk, take a day off and do something totally different, take an evening and read mysteries, or do something else you really enjoy.

2. Forgive yourself and then assess if there's any damage you need to repair—actual or emotional. If you've offended or hurt others, say so and apologize.

3. Analyze your behavior to see what you can learn. These reactions to stress are your mind's way of saying, "Hey, pay attention, you're out of balance. There are things you are not taking care of." What are those things? What led up to this eruption? How might you deal differently with a similar situation in the future?

4. Use other aspects of your personality to help you restore balance. Some people find using their other preferred function (the other middle letter in your type) helpful in understanding what has happened and restoring their more normal way of functioning.

   An ESTJ (dominant Extraverted Thinking) uses her Sensing to gather information about the sources of stress and the reality of her situation, which then allows her to get back in balance.

   An ENFP (dominant Extraverted Intuition) uses trusted people (Feeling) to help her begin to sort out what's real and to restore her normal perspective.

5. Talk over what happened with a trusted colleague or friend. This can help you see more clearly what happened. This is more likely to be an Extraverted strategy than an Introverted one.

   If you are an Introvert, you may find it more helpful

to reflect by yourself on the experience, perhaps to write it down. After that, you may find discussing it with another helpful.

Dealing with Others Who Are Highly Stressed

1. Do not try to reason with people when they are "in the grip," to help them see that they are being irrational. It doesn't work.
2. Do not make fun, joke, or try to tease them out of it. People don't have a sense of humor at such times. You might have been able to joke with them earlier, but not now.
3. Do suggest a break, such as a walk.
4. If the person seems to prefer Extraversion, he or she will most likely want to talk about it later with a trusted person, someone who will listen and be supportive.
5. If the person prefers Introversion, he or she will need some space and uninterrupted time to get back in balance. You may be able to help by protecting his or her time and space.
6. Realize that this eruption by another person is their issue, not yours, and protect yourself by getting out of the way, physically if necessary. You do not need to stay around and be abused.
7. Recognize that while type may play a part in identifying what is stressful and in describing the typical behaviors of stressed people, it is only part of the picture. (Remember our list of work stressors at the beginning of this chapter.)

Take care of yourself, remembering that this will mean different things for different types!

CHAPTER 10

MAKING THE MOST OF
YOUR TYPE AT WORK

We hope you've enjoyed reading the chapters, and that you've had some insights about yourself. You may even have had some insights about the people with whom you work. Now we want to give you some ideas about

1. using your type to its best advantage;
2. pushing yourself just beyond your comfort zone (oh no, not that!); and
3. applying some of the insights you've had

as a way of

1. improving your own sense of accomplishment in a difficult work environment;
2. gaining some new skills;
3. gaining some recognition for your improvements.

217

Let's look at some examples of people we have worked with who have used type knowledge to improve their work lives. Their development steps may give you some ideas about things you would like to try out.

Communication

Charlene was an ESTJ project assistant who usually worked with the same group of people, and she seemed to communicate well with them. Every once in a while she would be assigned to help out in another area, and it seemed that whenever that happened, she had difficulty communicating. It was frustrating for her and for those she was assisting.

She approached the problem logically (she is a Thinking type, after all), and decided the *WORKTypes* chapter on communications might help her. As a Sensing type, she needed to get started based on something tangible.

In reading through the communication chapter, she realized that in her own area people knew her well and felt connected with her personally. They had gotten used to her task focus and found it productive. However, whenever she was assigned to a new area, the people there seemed to perceive her focus as cold and uncollaborative. She realized that this got in the way of getting her work done efficiently (she needed a reason to change), so she had better do something about it (besides leaving copies of *WORKTypes* in each department!).

She developed a reminder sheet for herself, listing ways she wanted to adjust her normal communication style to be more effective. Her sheet looked like this:

Improving My Communication

PROJECT: COLLEAGUE:

1. Get to know the person. (Use their name. Ask about a picture on their desk. Talk about their work.)

2. Wait. Ask for their thoughts and ideas before I give mine.

3. Talk about any concern I have about the project, including how it might affect people (prepare this ahead of time—I'm not quick on my feet with this Feeling stuff).

4. *Together*, agree on deadlines, next steps, and how frequently we communicate.

She put copies of her list, with a place to record the other person's responses, in each project file. She knew if she didn't make this part of her routine, she could get caught up in conversations using her natural way and forget to round out her communication style.

Charlene also looked for a one-day course or seminar on

communication skills, one that was based on real issues and practical solutions, not theories. She likes practical courses that she can readily apply.

She also decided to ask for help. Her good friend Susan attends some project meetings with her, so she asked Susan to make note of any communications problems she observed (Thinking types often focus on the problems, the "bad" stuff). Susan agreed to help but said she also wanted to point out the good communications and especially the improvements she saw. Because Susan is comfortable communicating in ways that Charlene is not, Susan agreed that if she saw Charlene miscommunicate, she would step in and help clarify things.

Below is a recap of ways to improve your communication.

Using Type in Communication

1. Recognize your own natural style and the impact it may have on others—both positive and negative.
2. Work to modify your natural style so that others fully understand your message instead of getting hung up on your method.
3. Don't feel you have to do this alone. Ask others for information about the impact of your communication, for suggestions about what would make your communication more effective for them, and for feedback on your attempts to modify your style.
4. Remember others' positive motivations, what they potentially have to contribute to your work.
5. Take responsibility for finding ways to get the kind of communication you need—how you can ask questions of a particular person without making them feel defensive, how you can offer input and alternative suggestions in a positive way, etc.

Conflict

Judy and Maria had been partners for nine years, running a successful small business that offered a range of computer services. Judy, ENFJ, found herself feeling somewhat bored; she wanted to pursue some new interests. She thought that since she only needed to be at the office four days a week, perhaps she could find something new to do on the fifth day. She decided not to mention this to her partner, saying to herself that she didn't want to hurt Maria's feelings. Underneath, Judy was hoping to avoid any conflict with Maria.

Maria, ISTJ, was very pleased with the success of the business and with the utilizing and refining of her skills as time progressed. She was strongly committed to the partnership and the business, demonstrating the loyalty that is a hallmark of her type.

Judy located a work-from-the-home start-up business that seemed to fit comfortably with the one day a week she had free. Unfortunately, she didn't fully take into account her type.

Let's look at type in action in this scenario:

Judy

- ENFJ—known for enthusiastic involvement (and sometimes overcommitment)
- N = caught up in the new possibilities
- F = avoiding the possible conflicts

Maria

- ISTJ—known for focused, long-term commitments (and sometimes for protecting the status quo)
- S = focused on the data of success in the small business
- T = not noticing Judy's boredom
- T = thinking that all was well; it's only logical, isn't it!

Type played itself out. Soon Judy was taking time off to work on the new venture, leaving early, taking new business calls at the old business place. She had not used her Sensing or Thinking to see the reality of time and energy constraints, to anticipate how her interest in the exciting new work would draw her, or to recognize the logical consequences. Maria began to notice that Judy was avoiding her—something seemed wrong. Then their secretary came to Maria and told her about the telephone calls. Maria was stunned: Her loyalty and her principles seemed threatened, as well as the future of the business. She felt betrayed.

Maria stormed into Judy's office demanding to know what was going on. Each was convinced she was morally right, both were emotional—they knew they needed help!

The consultant they called in used the concept of type to help them see how each of their types helped them and got in their way. Each had a chance to state her perspective, to understand the other's, to explore their positions, to step into each other's shoes, and finally to assess where the partnership was. They decided to end it, but were able to do that with appreciation for each other and for the work they had done together.

The following is a recap of steps to use in resolving conflict.

Resolving Conflicts with Myers's Constructive Use of Differences

1. Recognize and understand your own perspective, with its strengths and its limitations.
2. Listen to and try to understand the other person within his or her own framework and motivation instead of attributing motive from your viewpoint.
3. Recognize the value of the other's goal and the potential contributions of the other outlook.
4. Ask questions to develop your understanding of the other's position and perspective.
5. Seek a solution that incorporates both people's goals, that meets the essential needs of both.

Time Management

Rachel, an ENFP, was on top of the world—she had just received a promotion and was being transferred to a new department! Her boss said he would miss her: She'd been providing training and meeting facilitation for the whole division, and everyone liked her style, her friendliness, and her creative help with their problems. The job had grown with her; she was always on the run and accomplished a lot. Of course it was true that her office was filled with piles of handouts and Post-it notes, but she always delivered what her clients asked.

Her new position was to plan, coordinate, and assess the training being delivered in the division to which she was transferred. She was to manage the five people in her group, their work and hers! She was filled with enthusiasm and ideas.

Three months later, Rachel was called in by her new boss for a three-month review. She looked forward to this with enthusiasm, as she thought about the new ideas she'd helped get under way, the new programs, and the camaraderie she'd developed with her group. She was totally unprepared for the serious critique her boss delivered. Her evaluation included the following negative comments about Rachel:

1. She was overextended, taking on too much of the actual training herself.
2. Her monthly reports were late, too brief, and too general.
3. She didn't return her calls in a timely fashion.
4. She was over budget.

Rachel was stunned. Her boss was right about those four points, she grudgingly admitted, but what about all the good things she had done? Rachel's boss said she wanted to see some improvement in thirty days. She would be monitoring Rachel's work and they would meet again.

Rachel was totally dejected by the feedback. She knew she'd always had difficulty with time and schedules, but it hadn't ever reared its head like it had now. She called her good friend Neal and told him about her evaluation. After listening, Neal said, "Sounds like your type just got caught!" Rachel realized he was right—she knew about type and liked her type description, but she also realized that some of her type preferences might be getting in her way in her new job.

That evening, she and Neal met for dinner and he gave her *WORKTypes,* saying, "Read Chapter Four." After he went home, Rachel read about time management and type and realized that she had been relying only on her strengths—her ideas, her creative training, her on-the-run planning, and her "just-in-time" finishes. She also realized she had not been paying attention to the less (for her) interesting parts of the job: schedules, time management, reports, tight turnaround in calls (and all were important to her boss).

The next morning she asked her staff to meet with her at the end of the day to discuss the problems they saw in the department. The staff said, "We love your energy and ideas—you're fun to be with—*but* we can't ever find you, you haven't given us our reviews, and we wish you'd slow down!"

Rachel explained her ENFP type and asked for help. They all energetically entered into helping her come up with a plan. Rachel thought it was a good one and worth trying, though she realized that the suggestions would challenge her:

Challenge #1: Cut down the number of training sessions she led. That was hard! Hands-on work and interaction with others were energizing for her.

Challenge #2: Commit to a one-day turnaround on phone calls. Prioritizing on the run was how she preferred to operate. It seemed difficult to have a "rule" to follow, even one she made herself. It helped when her secretary told her how disappointed people were when she didn't call back (appealing to her Feeling part).

Challenge #3: Since she just couldn't sit and write—there were so many more interesting things to do!—her forty-five-minute commute now has a contribution to make. She uses the time to talk into the tape recorder, "writing" her staff reviews and reports verbally.

Her office is still a mess—the walls are full of out-of-date Post-it notes—but she's more accessible, more timely in calls and reports, and is thinking she might find the next review a lot more positive.

The following is a recap of steps to follow to manage your time better.

Improving Time Management through Using Type

1. Become knowledgeable about your personality and time-management style; learn what works for you and what doesn't.
2. Seek information from others on the impact of your time-management style on them.
3. Be clear in communicating your style to others who are affected by it.
4. You may have to ask for what you need and negotiate for what's possible.
5. Set up some props to help yourself in your weak spots, such as a calendar system that works for you.
6. If your style works for you and doesn't negatively impact others, keep it.

Meetings

Kay, an ESFJ, was in the midst of "meeting madness" in her work area. She was a very positive person who hated disharmony and really worked at finding the best in any situation; but she found that, even with all her positive thinking, her encouragement of others, her focus on being a responsible team player—even with all that—she finally had to admit that the meetings in her department were just awful! Everyone complained, people came late and left early, there was little participation, few things were accomplished in them, and frustration reigned.

After reading the chapter on meetings, Kay pulled a couple of colleagues together and asked to do some brainstorming with them about their meetings. This was Kay's first challenge; as a dominant Feeling type, it was a stretch for her to identify the meetings as a problem to be solved. It might hurt her boss's feelings or seem disloyal. She needed to draw on her Thinking part.

She and her colleagues identified a number of type-related problems in their meetings. Then Kay, with the support of her colleagues, developed a proposal for her boss that said she would be responsible for the departmental meetings for the next three months—with some measurement in place to track improvements. Kay had met the second challenge—her assertiveness and action stretched her usual accommodating parts, and the measurement aspect was another example of development of her Thinking.

After acceptance by her boss, who was delighted to get out from under the burden of meetings, Kay gave everyone a one-page survey of how people would currently rate their department meetings, with space for suggestions. Kay didn't like to focus on the negative, but knew she needed this additional information. She then announced that she was going to be the meeting facilitator and would be adding in new ways to make the meetings work better. Kay used her type, ESFJ, to get things started, but also to gather data on how people felt, and to come to a conclusion about a way to make things better.

Kay is now working to respond to her colleagues' suggestions and make the meetings more productive and enjoyable. She really likes the following recap of steps to having better meetings.

Using Type in Meeting Management

1. Step back to analyze what's missing in your group meetings as we did in our scenario. Type knowledge can help identify some of the missing perspectives.

2. Take type into consideration before the meeting (sending out notices about topics), during the meeting (setting clear priorities, agreeing on time frames), and after the meeting (including follow-up plans) to insure that they are most productive for everyone.

3. Good meetings need to allow for the perspectives and contributions of all eight preferences. Groups need action *and* reflection, data *and* possibilities, logic *and* the impact on people, closure *and* openness.

4. Even if your group does not include people with all eight of the preferences, you will function better if all eight preferences and their perspectives are included; for example, if your group is all Thinkers, they will still make better decisions if they learn to ask, "What will be the impact of this on people?" and to pay attention to the answer.

5. When you are the one leading the meeting, assess your own skills so that you know your own strengths and shortcomings and how they relate to those at the meeting. Know where you might get sidetracked and identify ways you can use type to help you have a more productive meeting.

Leading

Mark, an ISTJ, was a manager of computer installations. However, the glory days of the department, the time when they installed huge mainframes for major companies, were over. His company had shifted to the personal computer market, and this meant a different kind of installation that was more customer oriented and individually focused.

Instead of expanding rapidly, his company was downsizing. Mark saw absenteeism going up, lower productivity, and low morale. He had gotten a directive from his manager to shape up the department.

Mark's wife, an ENFP, had listened to his worries about work. Always one to generate alternative possibilities, she had learned about type and suggested he might find some useful things in it for the current situation. ISTJs usually prefer to learn about new things when they can see practical applications, so Mark took her advice.

Mark carefully read the chapter on leading and saw himself jumping off the pages. He recalled his performance reviews (ISTJs like historical data), which described his strong organization and structure, his consistency, his ability to implement, his following of company policies, and his careful documentation. He also saw his "developmental needs" staring back at him: his lack of communication, especially with his staff; his bluntness, his occasional inflexibility; and his reluctance to make quick changes.

Mark decided to take advantage of the difficult situation he was in at work and to use his structured (STJ) nature to make some changes in his leadership style. On three-by-five cards he could carry in his shirt pocket, he listed questions he normally didn't ask. He wanted to develop his Intuitive skills so he included some N questions like, What's another way we could see this situation? What are some new ideas in our field?

He also wanted to work on his Feeling side and include people more. He made a list of his department members on his weekly "to do" list and he set a goal of checking in with them informally twice a week. (As an ISJ, his natural style had been to meet at more scheduled times.) He also decided to give each person at least one compliment a week, and he'd note that next to their name on his list. (As a Thinking type, he had been better at telling them what had gone wrong than what had gone right.)

He wanted to try these changes a step at a time, and he was likely to be more successful that way, given his type.

He didn't feel comfortable announcing these goals to others except his spouse. He wanted to try them on his own. He and his wife agreed to talk over his week and how it had gone every Saturday night. (He needed Friday night to relax quietly, not to talk, after his busy week. His spouse finally understood this need after learning about Extraversion and Introversion.) She liked being included in the process that would help him develop, and he found her insights about people helpful. She even suggested ways he might word things to others so that they would appear less blunt.

Mark still measured his success by evaluating quantitative data—absenteeism, productivity, and so on—but also began looking at qualitative measures, such as people seeming happier in their work. Ultimately his reward will be a more productive department.

The following is a recap of steps to follow to improve your ability to lead and to follow.

Important Points About Leading, Following, and Type

When you are leading, remember:

1. You likely have a preferred style.
2. Being aware of the strengths and limitations of that style may help you avoid mistakes.
3. You may need to take into account the needs of your followers so that they can work better with you.
4. You may need to actively include the use of all the preferences in your decision-making, whether that means making a conscious effort to ask the questions that preference would ask or seeking out people of those preferences.

When you are following, remember:

1. You also likely have a preferred style.
2. Being aware of your type may help you identify more of what you need from your leader.
3. Understanding your leader's style may help you approach your leader in a way that makes it easier for him or her to understand you.
4. Be aware that differences between your type and your leader's type are to be expected and can be managed to the advantage of both parties.

Teamwork

Matt, INTP, had always wanted to work in a particular department, known for its high-tech and cutting-edge focus. He was elated when he was selected for a lateral move into that department and felt highly motivated to get to work. On his first day, he found that his previous style of working independently was not the style used in this work unit. It was a very close-knit team—they met every morning to check in with each other and plan for the day, they socialized frequently after work, and they regularly stopped by each other's work areas.

After the first week, Matt was not only exhausted but questioning the move he'd made. His teammates were also wondering about his fit with the team.

In his next trip to the bookstore seeking some solace and quiet, he came upon *WORKTypes*. He'd learned about type theory on the Internet and then took the inventory several years ago in a class offered by Human Resources. He decided maybe the concept of type might help in his current situation, so he read the chapter on teams. He smiled to himself when he read about Introverts and how they prefer working on their own and like written rather than face-to-face communication. His style was a startling contrast to the practices of his new teammates, who appeared to be Extraverted. He knew that once he got to know them all, he'd feel easier about interacting, but in the beginning they seemed superficial and overly talkative. There was his own type bias, laid out on the page right in front of him. What irony: the right job and the wrong people.

As an INTP, he wanted to be able to give clear, logical analyses of core issues and tasks, but it felt like his teammates never gave him the chance! He decided to take the book back to the team. Maybe it could help.

The following are some steps to use in teamwork.

Tips for Teamwork and Type

1. Start with yourself.
   - What do you like to contribute?
   - What are your type biases?
2. Since teamwork requires some compromise, identify your real priorities.
   - What's most important to you?
   - What are you willing to negotiate?
3. Help your team carve out working agreements.
4. As problems occur, continue using your knowledge of type to identify sources of and solutions to problems.
5. Apply type not just to relationship issues, but also to problem-solving issues to make sure you've covered all the bases.
6. Laugh at your differences instead of being annoyed by them.

Change

Elaine is the ISFJ department head of the support staff in a large organization that is caught up in the same changes that everyone is today. Her group had not been in the mainstream of change, but then Elaine's boss called her in and said, "The division vice-president has decided the following changes will need to be made in your department and with your employees. You've got about a month to deliver on these changes." Elaine's stomach flipped as she read the list—it all seemed so radically different:

- All secretaries and executive assistants were now to have two groups to support instead of one.
- They were to be empowered to set their own schedules and priorities based on the needs of their two groups.
- Elaine's role was changing to one of resource allocation, budget management, and assessment of training needs.

Elaine spent several days just thinking about the changes; she found herself opening her top drawer and reading the list, then shutting the drawer again and shuddering. She worried about how people would react, whether they could do it, and how she could change herself. There were so many new skills to be learned.

Elaine recalled that she'd read our book and there was a chapter on change. She reread it and found several things that seemed to offer a lifeline. One line jumped out at her: "Recognize the role of the past." She realized two things: She'd been an effective and well-liked department head for the past five years; and she knew what had worked in motivating her group in the past and that neither of these things had changed. She had a base to operate from. The clamp on her mind loosened a little.

The second line she saw was: "What specifically needs to be changed for us to be successful?" The word *specifically* helped—she read through each of the changes and wrote down exactly what would need to be added and what would stay the same.

She then decided to look at what she'd learned about her type—she knew that ISFJs need realistic reasons, practical data, to have a plan and to receive support.

She realized that for three days she'd been Introverting and sorting. The reason for the changes was plain and simple: The division VP had said so! Now she needed help in looking at the practical steps everyone would need to take, and in putting together a plan on such short notice.

Challenge #1. Elaine decided to call a meeting of the department to present the changes and form some task-force groups to work on the challenges of the changes. That was a stretch for her. She really wanted to work it out by herself, but there wasn't time. It felt scary, but Elaine planned the meeting well. She ordered a good lunch for everyone and set up the room so groups could work on the problems after they ate. She made some charts of the requested changes and the thoughts she'd had.

Challenge #2. Elaine wasn't used to presenting information to the whole group; their meetings in the past had been pretty cut and dried. She drew on her experience of training sessions she'd attended and tried out some new techniques:

1. She listed the steps in dealing with change from the book.
2. She listed the steps in their work she had thought about.
3. She planned to have each of three groups work on one of the changes and then present to the whole group.

She was worried, stressed, and a little bit hopeful.

The feedback to Elaine after the meeting was positive, all in all. People were surprised at how helpful it was to talk about the changes with everyone and to be included in planning the steps to make the changes. At the end of thirty days, the department invited Elaine's boss in to review their plans. He was pleased and gave them some further input. Elaine and her staff were moving forward. There were some minor blocks, but everyone could help and did.

The following is a recap of steps to help you handle change in the workplace.

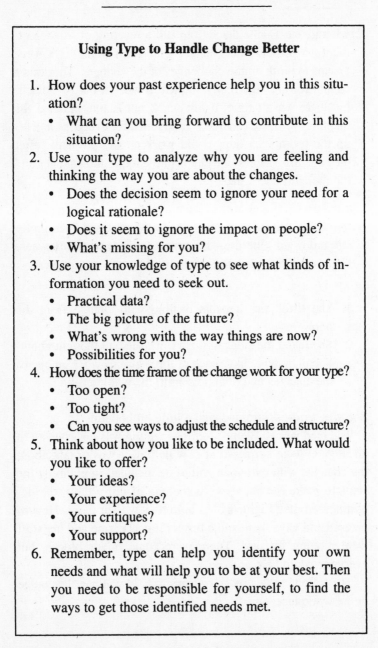

Using Type to Handle Change Better

1. How does your past experience help you in this situation?
   - What can you bring forward to contribute in this situation?
2. Use your type to analyze why you are feeling and thinking the way you are about the changes.
   - Does the decision seem to ignore your need for a logical rationale?
   - Does it seem to ignore the impact on people?
   - What's missing for you?
3. Use your knowledge of type to see what kinds of information you need to seek out.
   - Practical data?
   - The big picture of the future?
   - What's wrong with the way things are now?
   - Possibilities for you?
4. How does the time frame of the change work for your type?
   - Too open?
   - Too tight?
   - Can you see ways to adjust the schedule and structure?
5. Think about how you like to be included. What would you like to offer?
   - Your ideas?
   - Your experience?
   - Your critiques?
   - Your support?
6. Remember, type can help you identify your own needs and what will help you to be at your best. Then you need to be responsible for yourself, to find the ways to get those identified needs met.

Stress

Evelyn, ENTP, was the highest-ranking woman in a financial services organization and headed a division of 1,250 people. She was an achiever who described herself as having two speeds: "fast" and "faster." She had reorganized her department, making it a leader in its field, and had brought in talented people to help her run her department.

Her job and the organization were a wonderful fit for her personality type:

- She had constant interaction with people (E).
- She continually looked for new ways to do the work of her area and keep it on the cutting edge (N).
- She could critique and problem-solve (T).
- And while her P could be problematical at times because there were tight deadlines, on the other hand there was much change in her work, crises to handle, and variety to experience.

Evelyn, however, had a number of very serious issues to handle quickly: A few people weren't performing well and she had to terminate them, even though two were her friends. Changes in government regulations were forcing massive and quick changes in her division, and there was not enough time to explore options. Her personal stress built and she became ill; yet with important work to be done, she took very little time off. She found herself getting scattered among the possibilities and then swamped by them. She seemed unable to make decisions (luckily, her competent staff kept making them so that the division did not suffer). Usually enthusiastic about ideas, both hers and others, she began to go up and down in her moods. Her husband took the brunt of these, but others around her began to get concerned. She was showing exaggerated Intuition.

She totally ignored her illness (*EN*s don't pay much attention to bodily aches and pains). She developed terrible stomach pains, and when she was unable to eat, she finally had to take notice. If she didn't change her lifestyle, according to her physician, she would lose her ability to function at anything.

She went into the grip of her inferior function, Introverted Sensing. At first she focused on one fact: The division could not function without her. Then she moved on to another incorrect assumption: She could never work again. She even knew type well but didn't use any of that knowledge, either.

Her challenge was to get back in balance. She found suggestions in the chapter on stress. She took a leave of absence (resigning was too final a step at that point, and ruled out an option she wanted). She logically analyzed how she was feeling physically every day and concluded she felt too good to get back into that stressful job, no matter how much she had enjoyed it and its pay and prestige. She continued to talk over her options with good friends, and decided to try some short-term consulting positions where she could use her expertise and feel competent. Also, she could control her schedule. She finally admitted that long hours were not good for her health. She did make another decision: She resigned and seems at peace with that. (Her Judging friends said they knew she'd come to that decision, but she needed to do it in her own time.)

She is now using her awareness of her ENTP personality again to search for ways to handle her health and to contribute and work:

- She now pays attention to how she's feeling and has learned the value of time away from work.
- She has forgiven herself and apologized to those she needed to for her earlier outbreaks.

- She is learning she can't do it all and have her health; her Sensing can help her stay in balance.
- She is paying attention to her Feeling side and has decided to look for ways she can give back to her community.
- She keeps in touch with her friends and continues to get their input into looking at her career options.

The following are steps to help you handle the stress in your life, both your own and others.

Handling Stress Using Type

Helping Yourself
1. Pay attention—you really need a break.
2. Forgive yourself and then assess if there's any damage you need to repair, actual or emotional. Say you're sorry to yourself and others as needed.
3. Analyze your behavior to see what you can learn. It's your mind's way of saying, "Hey, pay attention! You're out of balance; there are things you are not taking care of."
4. Use other aspects of your personality to help you restore balance. Some people find using their other preferred function (the other middle letter in your type) helpful in understanding what has happened and restoring their more normal way of functioning.
5. Talk over what happened with a trusted colleague or friend. This can be helpful both in making clear that you are not a terrible person, and in helping you see more clearly what happened.

If you are working with someone as stressed as Evelyn, here are some tips.

Handling Stress Using Type

Dealing with Others

1. Do not try to reason with people when they are "in the grip," to help them see that they are being irrational—it doesn't work.
2. Do not make fun, joke, or try to tease them out of it—people don't have a sense of humor at such times. You might have been able to joke with them earlier, but not now.
3. Do suggest a break, such as a walk.
4. If the person seems to prefer Extraversion, he or she will most likely want to talk about the problem with a trusted person, someone who will listen and be supportive.
5. If the person prefers Introversion, he or she will need some space and uninterrupted time to get back in balance. You may be able to help by protecting his or her time and space.
6. Realize that this eruption by another person is their issue, not yours, and protect yourself by getting out of the way, physically if necessary. You do not need to stay around and be abused.
7. Recognize that while type may play a part in identifying what is stressful and in describing the typical behaviors of stressed people, it is only part of the picture.

Summary

The people in each of our examples faced very different issues and challenges, but they have some things in common. The strategies that they used can also be helpful to you in making the most of your type at work.

- They took objective looks at themselves—they weren't shy about looking at their type strengths and limitations.
- In some cases, they analyzed their job activities and even what the organization seemed to reward in terms of type behaviors.
- They decided what they wanted to build on in their personalities. For example, our STJs found that the structure in their personalities helped them make some needed changes. Our ENTP used her Intuition to keep searching for options.
- They decided what they wanted to develop, often the less-preferred parts of themselves, those letters not showing in their types. Some may adopt new behaviors; for example, the Thinker who decided to do community work; the Feeler developing critiquing skills; the Intuitive developing ways to handle details; the Sensor generating new possibilities.
- They looked at methods to help them develop: classes, reading, contact with trusted colleagues, using consultants.
- They took action and tried new behaviors. The risk was worth it!
- They figured out ways to evaluate their successes: self-knowledge, concrete data, and feedback from colleagues and bosses.

- Most of all, they accepted responsibility for their own work satisfaction and took some risks. They moved from being victimized by their problems to practically dealing with them.

We hope you will use this information to be more effective—and more satisfied—in your work!

CONCLUSION

ork will always be with us in one form or another, although the nature of our jobs may change. In this book, we've given you ways to understand the common tasks of work, such as communicating, managing time, making meetings productive, handling conflict, dealing with change, leading, working on teams, and handling stress. We've also suggested a means—applying psychological type—to help make each task go more smoothly. Through utilizing type, communication can be enhanced, problems solved better, and your work done more easily.

Cautions in Applying Psychological Type

You have a type, and it can help you identify who you are, what you do well, and what you might need to do differently. It is not meant to be a stereotype and to box you into acting only in certain ways. It would be especially inappropriate if you used your type as an excuse to act in only one way and ignored other important tasks. For example, imagine what it might be like to work with someone who only Extraverts or only Introverts!

Keep in mind, too, that it is tempting to assume that your type is the best way to be *all* of the time. It is the best way for you to be much of the time, but at some point you will find yourself in a situation where acting according to your type will be the wrong thing to do. You need to have the flexibility to try out some of the perspectives and approaches of the other types, too.

Finally, remember that there is more to you and your work than your psychological type! You may even find yourself meeting someone of your same type who is difficult for you to like! Type is a helpful tool, but not *the* answer. Many other factors are at work, as well.

Additional Resources

We've listed resources in the "Further Reading" section at the end of this book to continue your understanding of type, and, of course the footnotes also point to more places to learn. Reading *LIFETypes* will provide you a general background as well. Remember that if you want to take the MBTI (or the MBTI Step II), you'll need to find a qualified professional in your human resources department, at a community college or university, in your church, or from a private practitioner.

The most important resource, however, is the knowledge you will gain as you and your colleagues begin respectfully discussing your similarities and differences at work. Opening up such discussions is one of the most valuable contrubutions of psychological type.

Constructive Use of Differences: An Example

As authors, we've used our type differences in writing this book.

- Jean Kummerow, with her ESTJ perspective, contributed clear, simple explanations, down-to-earth examples, and practical suggestions. She kept the book moving between our writing sessions together.
- Nancy Barger, with her ENFP perspective, contributed new ways of seeing things, ways of handling people issues with sensitivity, and a focus on creating a healthier workplace. She helped move us on to a new and fun direction when we were stuck.
- Linda Kirby, as an INTP, provided ways of presenting complex material clearly, a logical framework, and the right word at the right time. She kept on task, creating and writing the book when Jean and Nancy lost focus.

The goal of this book is to help you also apply Isabel Myers's constructive use of differences by:

1. understanding your own type;
2. becoming aware of type differences;
3. learning about the other preferences;
4. acknowledging and respecting the value of other viewpoints;
5. seeking them out; and
6. incorporating those different perspectives into your own regular day-to-day work processes.

Good luck!

NOTES

Introduction

1 John L. Holland, "Exploring Careers with a Typology: What We Have Learned and Some New Directions," *American Psychologist*, 1996 (51), pp. 397–406.
2 Sandra Hirsh and Jean Kummerow, *LIFETypes* (New York: Warner Books, 1989).

Chapter 1: Introduction to Type

1 The material on the components of the MBTI was modified and reproduced by special permission of the Publisher, Consulting Psychologists Press, Palo Alto, CA 94303 from the *MBTI Step II Expanded Interpretive Report* by Naomi L. Quenk and Jean M. Kummerow. Copyright 1996 by Consulting Psychologists Press, Inc. All rights reserved. Further reproduction is prohibited without the publisher's written consent.
2 The short type descriptions are from Sandra Hirsh and

Jean Kummerow, *LIFETypes* (New York: Warner Books, 1989), pp. 71, 84, 96, 109, 121, 134, 146, 159, 172, 183, 195, 208, 220, 232, 245, 258. Used with permission.

Chapter 2: Communication and Conflict

1 Allen Hammer, "A Review of Selected Literature on the MBTI and Teams." Paper presented at Association for Psychological Type Conference (APT XI), July 1995, Kansas City, Missouri.
2 Ibid.

Chapter 3: Time Management

1 Personnel Decisions, Inc. *Successful Manager's Handbook* (Minneapolis: Personnel Decisions, Inc., 1992), pp. 90–99.

Chapter 4: Meetings

1 Personnel Decisions, Inc. *Successful Manager's Handbook* (Minneapolis: Personnel Decisions, Inc., 1992), p. 101.

Chapter 5: Leading: Being in Charge

1 Christa L. Walck, "Psychological Type and Management Research: A Review," *Journal of Psychological Type,* 1992 (24), pp. 13–23; and Linda K. Kirby, "Introduction," in *Developing Leaders* (Palo Alto, CA: Davies-Black, 1996).

2 Ushu C. V. Haley and Rosella Pini, "Blazing International Trails in Strategic Decision-Making Research." *Proceedings of The Myers-Briggs Type Indicator and Leadership: An International Research Conference* (College Park, MD: University of Maryland, 1994), pp. 19–30.

Chapter 6: Teamwork

1 A. L. Hammer, "A Review of Selected Literature on the MBTI and Teams." Paper presented at APT XI, July 1995, Kansas City, Missouri.

Chapter 7: Exploring Another Level of Type

1 Isabel Myers, *Gifts Differing* (Palo Alto, CA: Consulting Psychologists Press, 1980). See Chapters 1, 2, 8, 9, 15, 16, 17, and 18.

2 Isabel Briggs Myers and Mary H. McCaulley, *Manual: A Guide to the Development and Use of the Myers-Briggs Type Indicator* (Palo Alto, CA: Consulting Psychologists Press, 1985). See Chapter 3.

3 Katharine D. Myers and Linda K. Kirby, *Introduction to Type Dynamics and Development* (Palo Alto, CA: Consulting Psychologists Press, 1994).
4 Myers and McCaulley, op. cit., p. 18. Used with permission.

Chapter 8: Change

1 Nancy J. Barger, and Linda K. Kirby, *The Challenge of Change in Organizations: Helping Employees Thrive in the New Frontier* (Palo Alto, CA: Davies-Black, 1995).
2 Ibid. These authors have also developed a series of workshops on change from which this section is drawn.
3 Ibid. Table is adapted from Appendix "The Sixteen Types and Transitions" in *The Challenge of Change in Organizations: Helping Employees Thrive in the New Frontier* (Palo Alto, CA: Davies-Black, 1995), pp. 231–263. Used with permission.

Chapter 9: Stress

1 Naomi Quenk, *Beside Ourselves* (Palo Alto, CA: Consulting Psychologists Press, 1993).

FURTHER READING

Hirsh, Sandra, and Jean Kummerow, *LIFETypes*. New York: Warner Books, 1989.

Hirsh, Sandra, and Jean Kummerow, *Introduction to Type® in Organizations* (second edition). Palo Alto, CA: Consulting Psychologists Press, 1990.

Myers, Isabel Briggs. *Introduction to Type*, 5th edition. Palo Also, CA: Consulting Psychologists Press, 1993.

Additional resources on the MBTI Step II (formerly called the MBTI Expanded Analysis Report):

Kummerow, Jean M., and Naomi L. Quenk, *Interpretive Guide for the MBTI Expanded Analysis Report*. Palo Alto, CA: Consulting Psychologists Press, 1992.

Mitchell, Wayne D. *MBTI Step II Expanded Interpretive Report Manual*. Palo Alto, CA: Consulting Psychologists Press, 1997.

Saunders, David R. *Manual: MBTI Expanded Analysis Report*. Palo Alto, CA: Consulting Psychologists Press, 1989.

In addition, many excellent type-related resources are cited in the Notes.

ABOUT THE AUTHORS

JEAN M. KUMMEROW, PH.D., is a consulting psychologist headquartered in St. Paul, Minnesota. She has an international practice specializing in leadership/management development, career counseling, team building, and training professionals in the use of psychological instruments. She is staff psychologist for the Blandin Foundation's Community Leadership Program to develop rural leaders in Minnesota and is the coauthor of *Introduction to Type in Organizations, LIFETypes*, career counseling guides, and MBTI Step II materials.

NANCY J. BARGER, M.A., is a consultant to leaders and organizations, especially those undergoing change. She delivers organizational change and MBTI training programs in the United Kingdom, Canada, New Zealand, Australia, Singapore, and across the U.S. She is a member of the International Faculty of the Association for Psychological Type MBTI Qualifying Training Program, and is past president of the Association for Psychological Type.

LINDA K. KIRBY, PH.D., is a writer, editor, and trainer specializing in use of the Myers-Briggs Type Indicator. She is coeditor of *Introduction to Type* and *Developing Leaders*, and coauthor of *Introduction to Type Dynamics and Development.* Kirby also delivers organizational change consulting with Barger. She is currently director of the Association for Psychological Type MBTI Qualifying Training Program.

BARGER AND **KIRBY** are coauthors of *The Challenge of Change in Organizations: Helping Employees Thrive in the New Frontier*, which was short-listed for the Ben Franklin Best of Business Books in 1995 Award.